All-Star 2025
The Game That Defined a Generation

Introduction

Video games have always been more than a pastime. They are immersive experiences that shape culture, define generations, and bring people together in ways no other form of entertainment can. All-Star 2025 was not just another entry in the gaming industry—it was a phenomenon that redefined interactive entertainment, setting a new benchmark for what video games could achieve. From the moment it was announced, it captured the imagination of millions, creating a level of anticipation rarely seen before in the gaming world. When it finally launched, it did not just meet expectations; it shattered them, leaving an indelible mark on gaming history.

This was not a game designed merely to entertain—it was built to evolve, to push boundaries, and to immerse players in an experience that felt as limitless as their imagination. Its foundation lay in innovation. With unparalleled graphics powered by cutting-edge game engines, AI-driven opponents that adapted to player behavior, and an open-world structure that blended seamlessly with competitive multiplayer modes, All-Star 2025 was the perfect fusion of technology, strategy, and storytelling. Unlike anything before it, the game offered a level of realism and interactivity that made every match feel dynamic and unpredictable.

At its core, All-Star 2025 was about competition, but it was also about connection. It fostered an ecosystem where players were no longer just participants—they were creators, strategists, and performers on a global stage. Social media exploded with highlights of epic plays, streamers built careers around mastering its mechanics, and esports organizations quickly recognized it as the next big thing.

It was not simply a game—it was a movement, an entire subculture that shaped conversations in gaming forums, live-streaming platforms, and even mainstream media.

But with success came challenges. All-Star 2025 found itself at the center of heated debates about gaming ethics, microtransactions, and competitive integrity. Some critics argued that its approach to monetization blurred the line between fairness and pay-to-win mechanics, while others pointed to its impact on the growing esports industry, questioning whether professional gaming was evolving too fast for its own good. Yet, despite the controversies, one thing remained undeniable—this game had changed the industry forever.

Beyond gaming, All-Star 2025 became a cultural touchstone. Its impact could be seen in music collaborations, fashion crossovers, and cinematic storytelling. Brands clamored to be associated with it, recognizing the massive influence it had on younger audiences. The game's characters and lore extended beyond the screen, inspiring fan fiction, digital art, and even animated adaptations. It was more than a game—it was an experience that transcended entertainment and became a defining part of modern digital culture.

This book is an exploration of how All-Star 2025 became the game that defined a generation. From its inception and groundbreaking technology to its rise in esports and the passionate community that fueled its success, we will take a deep dive into the elements that made it legendary. Whether you are a longtime player, a casual fan, or simply someone curious about how one game could leave such a profound impact, this journey will provide insights into an era where gaming was not just something people did—it was something they lived.

Chapter 1
The Genesis of All-Star 2025

Every great game begins with an idea, but All-Star 2025 was never just an idea—it was a vision. A vision to create something groundbreaking, something that would not only entertain but redefine gaming as an experience. It wasn't born out of market trends or corporate strategies; it emerged from a passion to craft a game that would challenge the limits of technology and human creativity. This chapter delves into the origins of All-Star 2025, tracing its journey from a mere concept to a global gaming sensation.

The story begins in a small but ambitious development studio where a group of visionaries, programmers, and designers shared a dream: to create a game that would revolutionize competitive gaming. At the heart of this ambition was the belief that gaming was evolving beyond traditional entertainment—it was becoming a culture, a way of life, a platform where players didn't just consume content but actively shaped it. With that philosophy in mind, the team set out to develop something unlike anything before it: a game that combined skill-based mechanics with a living, breathing world that would change dynamically based on how players interacted with it.

The earliest brainstorming sessions for All-Star 2025 were filled with wild ideas, some too ambitious for existing technology to handle. But the developers were determined. They envisioned a game that would seamlessly integrate real-time decision-making, evolving AI opponents, and a physics engine so advanced that every movement, every strike, every action would feel intuitive yet unpredictable. The challenge was immense—creating a game that balanced strategy, action, and storytelling in a way that had never been done before.

One of the most critical moments in its development came when the team decided to break away from conventional game design norms. Instead of crafting a linear experience, they introduced an innovative AI system that would allow the game to evolve based on player behavior. Every match, every encounter, and every strategy deployed by a player would leave an imprint on the game's world, making it feel alive. This concept of a responsive, ever-changing game environment became one of All-Star 2025's defining features.

But innovation comes at a cost. Development faced numerous roadblocks, from funding challenges to technical limitations that seemed insurmountable. There were moments when the project nearly collapsed under its own weight, with skeptics questioning whether it could even be completed. However, the core team refused to back down. They doubled down on their vision, refining the game's mechanics, pushing technology to its limits, and assembling some of the best minds in the gaming industry to bring their dream to life.

As development progressed, word about All-Star 2025 began to spread. Leaks, teasers, and early concept trailers generated an unprecedented level of hype, drawing attention from both casual gamers and professional players eager to see how this ambitious project would unfold. By the time the first beta version was unveiled, it was clear that All-Star 2025 was more than just another title in the gaming industry—it was a revolution waiting to happen.

The genesis of All-Star 2025 is a testament to what happens when vision meets determination. It was not created in a vacuum but forged through years of trial and error, innovation, and a relentless pursuit of excellence. The journey of its creation is as compelling as the game itself, setting the stage for what would become one of the most defining gaming experiences of its generation.

From Concept to Reality

Every great game starts with a concept—an ambitious idea that exists only in the minds of its creators. But taking that concept and transforming it into a fully realized, playable experience is a monumental challenge. All-Star 2025 was not just another video game; it was a vision that sought to redefine the industry. Bringing it to life required a perfect balance of creativity, technical expertise, and unwavering determination.

The journey began with a simple yet powerful question: What would the ultimate gaming experience look like? The creators of All-Star 2025 didn't want to build just another competitive game; they wanted to create a world that was immersive, unpredictable, and endlessly engaging. They envisioned a title where every match felt unique, every decision had consequences, and players were not just participants but active architects of their own experience.

From the outset, the development team knew that innovation had to be at the core of All-Star 2025. They wanted to push boundaries, introduce never-before-seen mechanics, and craft a game that would remain relevant for years to come. However, ambition alone wasn't enough. They needed cutting-edge technology to support their vision. This led them to invest heavily in artificial intelligence, advanced physics engines, and real-time rendering techniques that could create an unparalleled level of realism.

One of the first major hurdles was designing the game's mechanics. The team debated for months on how to balance skill-based gameplay with an evolving AI system. They wanted a game where player actions would have lasting impacts, but they also needed to ensure that the experience remained fair and competitive. This led to the development of a groundbreaking AI-driven environment where NPCs learned from player behavior, strategies adapted in real time, and no two matches were ever the same.

Another critical challenge was world-building. The developers didn't just want a collection of maps—they wanted an interconnected universe. They meticulously designed a dynamic ecosystem where weather patterns, terrain changes, and real-time events influenced gameplay. This level of detail required unprecedented levels of collaboration between artists, engineers, and designers, pushing the limits of what was possible in game development.

Funding was another significant obstacle. Investors were skeptical about the project's scope, questioning whether such an ambitious game could ever be completed. There were moments when the future of All-Star 2025 seemed uncertain, with development costs spiraling and deadlines constantly shifting. But the team's belief in their vision never wavered. They turned to crowdfunding, securing a passionate community of backers who were eager to see the game become a reality. This grassroots support not only provided financial backing but also solidified All-Star 2025 as a game built for the players, by the players.

As development progressed, early prototypes were tested extensively. Feedback from professional gamers, streamers, and industry experts played a crucial role in refining mechanics and balancing gameplay. With each iteration, All-Star 2025 grew closer to perfection. When the first official trailer dropped, it took the gaming world by storm. The anticipation was palpable—players knew they were about to witness something extraordinary.

Turning a concept into reality is never easy, especially when that concept aims to revolutionize an industry. All-Star 2025 wasn't just the product of technology and design; it was a testament to passion, resilience, and the relentless pursuit of excellence. Its journey from an idea to a fully realized game is a story of vision meeting execution—an achievement that would leave an indelible mark on gaming history.

The Creative Minds Behind the Game

No great game is created in isolation. Behind every groundbreaking title is a team of visionaries—artists, designers, programmers, and strategists—who bring a concept to life. All-Star 2025 was no exception. It was the result of an extraordinary collaboration between some of the most talented individuals in the gaming industry, all united by a single goal: to create a game that would redefine competitive play and immersive storytelling.

At the helm of the project was Ethan Kade, the creative director and mastermind behind All-Star 2025. A former esports champion turned game developer, Kade had firsthand experience with the highs and lows of competitive gaming. He understood what players wanted—an experience that was not just skill-based but also dynamic and evolving. His vision was clear: All-Star 2025 wouldn't just be a game; it would be a battleground where strategy, adaptability, and mastery would define the best players in the world.

Joining him was Dr. Liana Chen, a leading expert in artificial intelligence and machine learning. Chen's expertise in AI-driven gameplay was instrumental in crafting the game's revolutionary NPCs, which could adapt to player behavior in real-time. Under her guidance, All-Star 2025 introduced an evolving AI ecosystem where no two matches ever felt the same. Whether players were battling AI opponents or engaging in dynamic team-based combat, the system ensured that every encounter was fresh, challenging, and engaging.

The game's art direction was spearheaded by Marco Alvarez, a veteran digital artist known for his work in cinematic storytelling. Alvarez envisioned a game world that was not just visually stunning but deeply immersive. Every landscape, character, and structure was designed with meticulous detail, making All-Star 2025 a visually striking experience. His work on the lighting engine, physics-based animations, and environmental textures ensured that the game set a new benchmark for realism in competitive gaming.

One of the most critical elements of the game was its sound design and musical score. Enter Diane Fraser, an award-winning composer known for her work in both film and interactive media. Fraser believed that audio was as crucial as visual elements in creating immersion. She crafted an adaptive soundtrack that responded to in-game events, ensuring that players felt every moment of tension, triumph, and defeat. Combined with realistic sound effects and immersive spatial audio, her work brought All-Star 2025 to life in a way that few games had achieved before.

Of course, none of this would have been possible without Nathan Bishop, the lead programmer and technical architect behind the game's infrastructure. His challenge was immense—designing a server architecture that could handle millions of concurrent players, ensuring seamless cross-platform functionality, and integrating cloud-based rendering for ultra-realistic visuals. Under his leadership, All-Star 2025 achieved unparalleled performance, allowing players from across the globe to engage in massive battles without lag or server crashes.

But beyond individual contributions, what truly made All-Star 2025 special was the synergy between these creative minds. Unlike many game development teams where different departments worked in isolation, this team operated as a unified force. Ideas were constantly exchanged, feedback loops were quick and effective, and every member was deeply involved in the game's evolution.

Their collective passion, expertise, and relentless pursuit of perfection turned All-Star 2025 from a dream into reality. It was more than just a project; it was a labor of love, a testament to what happens when the brightest minds in the industry come together with a shared purpose. Thanks to their creativity and dedication, All-Star 2025 didn't just enter the gaming world—it redefined it.

Early Challenges and Breakthroughs

Bringing All-Star 2025 to life was never going to be easy. The ambition behind the game was immense, and with great ambition came great obstacles. From technical constraints to financial struggles, the development team faced numerous roadblocks on their journey. Yet, for every challenge they encountered, there was an equally significant breakthrough that propelled the project forward. The early stages of development were a test of resilience, creativity, and problem-solving—qualities that ultimately shaped All-Star 2025 into the masterpiece it became.

One of the biggest challenges the team faced was pushing the limits of gaming technology. The vision for All-Star 2025 was clear: a seamless multiplayer experience, dynamic AI-driven gameplay, and unparalleled graphics. But the technology required to support this vision did not yet exist in a fully functional form. Traditional game engines struggled to handle the level of complexity the developers demanded. The solution? Instead of working within the limitations of existing tools, the team customized their own version of an advanced game engine, integrating AI-driven physics simulations and a unique rendering system that allowed for hyper-realistic textures and real-time environmental changes. This breakthrough laid the foundation for All-Star 2025's stunning visuals and fluid gameplay.

Another major hurdle was developing the AI system that would make every match feel unique. The idea was to create an AI that wasn't just reactive but proactive—one that could learn from player behavior and adjust its strategy accordingly. However, early prototypes failed to deliver the desired effect. Enemies were either too predictable or too erratic, making gameplay either too easy or frustratingly random. After months of trial and error, the breakthrough came when the development team implemented machine learning algorithms that allowed AI opponents to analyze player patterns over multiple matches. This innovation meant that no two encounters were ever the same—AI could adapt to player strategies, creating a challenge that felt natural rather than scripted.

Beyond technology, financial struggles threatened to derail the entire project. Developing a game of this magnitude required significant funding, and investors were hesitant. They saw the ambitious nature of All-Star 2025 as a risk rather than an opportunity. Initial funding was limited, forcing the team to work under tight constraints. Just when it seemed like the project might stall, the team turned to an alternative strategy—crowdfunding. By launching an early campaign and showcasing their prototype, they built a community of passionate supporters who believed in their vision. This financial breakthrough not only secured much-needed resources but also created an engaged fan base even before the game's release.

One of the final and most critical breakthroughs came with network optimization for online multiplayer. Large-scale multiplayer games often suffer from latency issues, leading to lag and unresponsive controls. Given that All-Star 2025 was meant to be a competitive game, any delay, even by milliseconds, could ruin the experience. After months of testing and failed solutions, the breakthrough arrived in the form of a revolutionary cloud-based server system that dynamically adjusted bandwidth based on player density. This ensured smooth, lag-free gameplay, even in massive online battles.

The road to All-Star 2025 was paved with obstacles, but the determination of its creators turned every setback into an opportunity for innovation. The game that emerged from these trials was not just a technological marvel but a testament to the power of perseverance. Every challenge was a lesson, and every breakthrough was a step closer to creating the game that would define a generation.

Setting the Stage for a Revolution

By the time All-Star 2025 was nearing completion, it had already become more than just a game—it was a movement. From its early conceptualization to its first playable prototypes, the game's potential was undeniable. But the real question was: could it truly redefine the gaming landscape? The answer would be revealed through a combination of strategic marketing, cutting-edge technology, and an engaged player community that was ready to embrace something revolutionary.

Unlike other competitive games that followed a predictable formula, All-Star 2025 was designed to challenge every norm in the industry. The developers were determined to create an experience that blurred the lines between competitive gaming, storytelling, and social interaction. They didn't just want to release a game; they wanted to set a new standard—one that would influence future titles for years to come.

A key factor in setting the stage for this revolution was the game's dynamic and evolving AI system. Traditional competitive games often relied on static mechanics, where players learned predictable patterns and optimized their strategies accordingly. In contrast, All-Star 2025 introduced AI that could learn and adapt, creating an unpredictable and ever-changing challenge. Whether players faced AI opponents or competed in player-versus-player (PvP) modes, the game's intelligent response system ensured that no two matches ever felt the same. This was a bold step toward making gaming more immersive, challenging, and deeply engaging.

Equally important was the game's seamless integration of virtual reality (VR) and augmented reality (AR). While many games experimented with these technologies in isolated ways, All-Star 2025 was designed to fully embrace them. Players could step into an AR-enhanced world where their in-game actions influenced the physical environment around them, or they could use VR to immerse themselves completely in high-stakes competitive battles. This fusion of real-world interaction and virtual gameplay was unlike anything seen before, positioning the game as a trailblazer in the gaming industry.

But technology alone wasn't enough to ignite a revolution. The developers knew that community engagement would be the driving force behind All-Star 2025's success. They didn't just want players to play the game; they wanted them to be part of the game's evolution. This meant incorporating player-driven narratives, where the collective actions of the gaming community influenced future updates, seasonal events, and even storyline developments. Players were not just competitors; they were co-creators of the All-Star 2025 universe.

To generate excitement, marketing for the game was carefully crafted to be an event in itself. Instead of traditional advertising, the team launched cryptic teaser campaigns, interactive ARG (alternate reality game) challenges, and live-streamed development updates. These strategies didn't just build hype; they made players feel like they were part of something bigger. The pre-release beta program allowed a select group of players to test and refine the game, fostering a sense of exclusivity and anticipation that spread like wildfire across social media platforms.

By the time the official launch date was announced, All-Star 2025 was not just another game hitting the market—it was an industry-defining moment. It represented a shift in how games were designed, played, and experienced. The stage was set for a revolution, and the gaming world was ready to witness history in the making.

Chapter 2
The Technology That Changed Gaming

The gaming industry has always been shaped by technological innovation, but few games have pushed the boundaries of what is possible quite like All-Star 2025. From its earliest stages of development, it was designed not just as a game, but as a technological revolution—a seamless fusion of cutting-edge graphics, AI-driven gameplay, and immersive real-time experiences. While many titles before it had introduced elements of innovation, All-Star 2025 took things a step further, combining the latest advancements into a singular, cohesive experience that redefined the future of gaming.

The developers knew that in order to create something groundbreaking, they would have to rethink how games were traditionally built. One of their primary objectives was to eliminate the limitations that had held back competitive gaming for years—lag, predictable AI behavior, static environments, and hardware constraints. This meant integrating a suite of technologies that had never been used together in a single game before. From advanced AI learning models to cloud-rendered graphics, every aspect of the game was developed with the future in mind.

A key innovation that set All-Star 2025 apart was its use of real-time adaptive AI. While traditional NPCs (non-playable characters) followed scripted behaviors, the AI in All-Star 2025 learned and evolved based on the actions of the players. This meant that no two matches ever felt the same. AI opponents adjusted their strategies dynamically, learning from previous encounters and becoming more formidable over time. The technology behind this was inspired by machine learning models used in robotics and cybersecurity, making the AI opponents as unpredictable and intelligent as human competitors.

Another game-changing feature was the integration of cloud-based rendering. For years, graphical fidelity had been tied to the limitations of individual gaming hardware. Players with high-end PCs or next-generation consoles had access to superior visuals, while those with older hardware were left behind. All-Star 2025 broke this cycle by leveraging cloud gaming infrastructure. This allowed players to experience ultra-high-definition graphics regardless of their local hardware capabilities, as the game's rendering was performed on powerful cloud servers and streamed in real-time to the player's device.

The game also redefined cross-platform compatibility. Unlike previous multiplayer titles that struggled with performance differences between PC, console, and mobile devices, All-Star 2025 was designed to offer a seamless experience across all platforms. Players could start a match on their gaming console, continue it on their VR headset, and later switch to a mobile device without losing progress. This level of fluid, device-independent gameplay was made possible through advanced networking algorithms and a universal game engine optimized for multiple devices.

Perhaps the most exciting aspect of All-Star 2025 was its integration of virtual and augmented reality. While many games had dabbled in VR and AR before, few had successfully merged them into competitive gameplay. All-Star 2025 provided an immersive, real-time gaming experience where VR players could battle against traditional screen players without any competitive disadvantage. Meanwhile, AR features allowed players to bring elements of the game into the real world, blurring the lines between digital and physical interaction.

By combining these breakthrough technologies into one cohesive system, All-Star 2025 set a new benchmark for the gaming industry. It was not just about better graphics or smarter AI—it was about creating a living, evolving gaming ecosystem that adapted to its players. As we explore the various technologies that made this possible, it becomes clear why All-Star 2025 wasn't just another game—it was the technology that changed gaming forever.

Unreal Engine and Photorealistic Graphics

One of the most defining aspects of All-Star 2025 was its breathtaking visual fidelity, powered by the industry-leading Unreal Engine. From the very beginning, the development team knew that if they wanted to create a game that would set new standards for realism and immersion, they needed an engine capable of delivering photorealistic graphics, real-time lighting effects, and seamless open-world rendering. Unreal Engine provided the perfect foundation for this ambitious vision, allowing the game to achieve a level of graphical detail and fluidity that had never been seen before in competitive gaming.

The use of Unreal Engine 5 in All-Star 2025 marked a technological leap forward. One of its most groundbreaking features was Nanite virtualized geometry, which allowed the game to render billions of polygons in real-time without compromising performance. This meant that every texture, character model, and environment was packed with an incredible level of detail, from the individual pores on a character's skin to the intricate patterns on armor and weapons. Instead of relying on traditional polygon budgets, Nanite allowed the developers to use cinematic-quality assets in gameplay, resulting in an unmatched level of realism.

Another major breakthrough was Lumen, Unreal Engine's fully dynamic global illumination system. In traditional games, lighting is often pre-baked, meaning shadows and reflections remain static regardless of changes in the environment. However, with Lumen, All-Star 2025 featured real-time lighting that dynamically reacted to player movements, environmental shifts, and time-of-day cycles. Whether it was the flickering glow of neon lights in an urban battle arena or the golden hues of a setting sun casting long shadows across a desert landscape, the lighting in All-Star 2025 felt natural and immersive.

One of the biggest challenges in developing hyper-realistic graphics was ensuring optimized performance across all platforms. The team leveraged temporal super-resolution (TSR), an advanced upscaling technology that allowed players on lower-end hardware to experience high-quality visuals without the need for expensive GPUs. This feature ensured that All-Star 2025 ran smoothly on a variety of devices, from next-generation consoles and high-end PCs to cloud gaming platforms, all while maintaining 4K resolution and high frame rates.

Character animation was another area where Unreal Engine played a crucial role. With the help of MetaHuman Creator, the development team was able to design lifelike characters with natural facial expressions, realistic body movements, and fluid animations. These advancements eliminated the stiffness commonly seen in video game characters, making every interaction—whether it was a high-speed chase, a melee battle, or an emotional cinematic sequence—feel organic and believable.

Additionally, All-Star 2025 leveraged Unreal Engine's Chaos Physics System, which introduced realistic destruction mechanics and environmental interactions. Buildings crumbled naturally under heavy fire, glass shattered dynamically, and debris scattered in a way that mirrored real-world physics. These details weren't just for aesthetics; they actively influenced gameplay, allowing players to use destructible environments as strategic tools during combat.

By harnessing the full power of Unreal Engine, All-Star 2025 delivered an unparalleled visual experience that blurred the line between gaming and reality. It wasn't just about creating a beautiful game—it was about immersing players in a world so lifelike that they felt like they were truly part of it. Through cutting-edge graphical technology, the game redefined the possibilities of interactive entertainment, setting a new gold standard for realism in the gaming industry.

AI-Powered NPCs: A New Level of Interaction

One of the most groundbreaking features of All-Star 2025 was its AI-powered NPCs (Non-Playable Characters), which brought a level of interaction, intelligence, and adaptability never before seen in gaming. Traditional NPCs in video games follow pre-scripted behavior patterns, making them predictable and often repetitive. In contrast, All-Star 2025 introduced a revolutionary AI system that allowed NPCs to learn, adapt, and react to player actions dynamically, creating a world that felt truly alive.

At the core of this innovation was machine learning and neural network integration, which enabled NPCs to process vast amounts of data in real-time. Instead of following static behaviors, these NPCs observed player movements, combat strategies, and decision-making patterns, allowing them to adjust their responses accordingly. This meant that no two encounters were ever the same—NPCs learned from each battle, developing new tactics and even predicting player strategies over time.

For example, in single-player and cooperative missions, enemy NPCs could analyze attack patterns and adapt mid-fight, countering repetitive moves instead of falling victim to the same tactics repeatedly. If a player relied too much on ranged combat, enemies would begin using cover more effectively or rush the player aggressively. If a player preferred stealth, NPC guards would start patrolling in unpredictable patterns or communicate with each other to set traps. This real-time adaptation made battles feel more engaging, requiring players to constantly evolve their playstyles rather than relying on a single winning strategy.

Another major advancement was the introduction of emotionally responsive NPCs, an AI system designed to simulate human-like personalities, emotions, and decision-making. NPC allies in All-Star 2025 didn't just react to player commands; they built relationships with the player based on previous interactions. If a player consistently supported a particular NPC in battle, that character would become more loyal, offering assistance in critical moments and even developing a unique dialogue arc. Conversely, if a player ignored or acted recklessly around an NPC, they might become hesitant to help, even refusing to assist in certain situations.

This emotional intelligence extended beyond friendly NPCs. Dynamic NPC dialogue and behavior allowed side characters and shopkeepers to recognize individual players, remembering past encounters and responding accordingly. If a player frequently visited a particular vendor, the NPC might offer discounts, rare items, or even engage in small talk about recent in-game events. This level of persistent memory made every interaction feel more personal, deepening immersion in the game world.

Additionally, All-Star 2025 introduced community-driven NPC behavior, where major in-game events influenced the actions of NPCs across the world. If a high-ranking NPC leader was assassinated in a multiplayer event, the game's factions would reorganize, resulting in new alliances, conflicts, and missions for players to engage with. These changes were not pre-scripted but generated in real-time based on player decisions, ensuring that the game world evolved naturally over time.

Perhaps the most ambitious feature was self-learning NPC trainers and opponents. In ranked matches, AI-driven competitors could be trained by real players, inheriting their strategies and playstyles. This meant that even when players were offline, their AI counterparts could continue competing, making matches unpredictable and constantly evolving.

By integrating these advanced AI systems, All-Star 2025 created an interactive world where NPCs felt just as intelligent and unpredictable as human players. The result was a dynamic, immersive experience that blurred the line between scripted game design and true artificial intelligence, setting a new benchmark for future gaming innovation.

VR, AR, and Mixed Reality Integration

One of the most revolutionary aspects of All-Star 2025 was its seamless integration of virtual reality (VR), augmented reality (AR), and mixed reality (MR), transforming the way players engaged with the game. While many games had experimented with these technologies separately, All-Star 2025 blended them into a single, immersive experience that allowed players to interact with the game world in ways never before possible. This integration was not just a gimmick; it fundamentally changed gameplay by offering deeper immersion, strategic depth, and accessibility across multiple platforms.

The VR experience in All-Star 2025 redefined what it meant to step inside a game. With full-body motion tracking and next-generation VR controllers, every movement—whether dodging an attack, swinging a melee weapon, or signaling a teammate—was reflected in real time. Unlike traditional VR games that often confined players to small environments, All-Star 2025 utilized procedural space optimization, allowing players to navigate vast battlefields without spatial limitations. Haptic feedback technology further enhanced the experience, making every action feel more lifelike. Players could feel the recoil of their weapons, the impact of an enemy's strike, and even the subtle vibrations of footsteps approaching from behind, making them hyper-aware of their surroundings in ways never before possible.

For players without VR headsets, All-Star 2025 introduced a sophisticated AR mode, which overlaid digital game elements onto real-world surroundings. This allowed players to turn their living rooms, backyards, or even city streets into active gaming environments. AR technology brought a new dimension to strategy, allowing real-time HUD displays to project stats, maps, and strategic overlays into a player's field of vision without breaking immersion. The ability to summon in-game objects, track enemy movements, or see real-time holographic teammates provided an unprecedented level of engagement. Competitive players could use AR to enhance their tactical awareness, seeing enemy movements displayed on walls, analyzing terrain advantages, or marking objectives in real-world spaces.

Mixed reality took this integration a step further by allowing players to interact with both the physical and digital worlds simultaneously. Players wearing MR headsets could see both their real environment and digital elements layered into it, ensuring that even real-world objects could become part of the gameplay experience. This was particularly groundbreaking in multiplayer scenarios, where MR players could physically take cover behind real-world objects while engaging in intense firefights with virtual opponents. The ability to interact with both VR and non-VR players in a seamless, cross-reality experience eliminated the traditional barriers between different gaming platforms.

The cross-platform nature of All-Star 2025 ensured that whether players were using a headset, a mobile device, or a gaming console, they could all participate in the same shared universe. The game's real-time synchronization technology allowed users across different realities to interact in meaningful ways, creating a truly inclusive and interconnected experience. This innovation was not just about making the game look impressive; it was about making the game feel alive, adapting to the player's chosen level of immersion.

By integrating VR, AR, and MR into a unified gaming experience, All-Star 2025 set a new benchmark for the future of interactive entertainment. It was no longer just about playing a game; it was about living inside one. The technology behind All-Star 2025 blurred the lines between the digital and physical worlds, proving that the next frontier of gaming was not confined to a single screen but expanded into the very reality players inhabited.

Cloud Gaming and Cross-Platform Play

One of the defining features that set All-Star 2025 apart from its predecessors was its seamless integration of cloud gaming and cross-platform play. While gaming had traditionally been tied to hardware limitations and platform restrictions, All-Star 2025 broke these barriers, creating a truly accessible experience for players across different devices. Whether playing on a high-end gaming PC, a next-generation console, or a mobile device, users could enjoy the same high-quality experience without being limited by their hardware. This revolution in gaming technology ensured that no player was left behind, regardless of the platform they chose.

Cloud gaming played a pivotal role in enabling this accessibility. Unlike traditional games that required powerful hardware to run high-resolution graphics and complex physics simulations, All-Star 2025 leveraged cloud-based rendering, allowing players to experience cutting-edge visuals without needing top-tier gaming rigs. The game's servers handled all the heavy processing, streaming the gameplay to users in real time. This eliminated long installation times, massive storage requirements, and hardware limitations, making it possible for even lower-end devices to run the game at ultra-high settings. The introduction of adaptive streaming technology ensured smooth gameplay, adjusting resolution and frame rates dynamically based on the player's internet connection. This meant that whether a player was on a fiber-optic broadband connection or using mobile data, they could still enjoy an optimal gaming experience without latency issues.

Cross-platform play was another game-changing innovation that made All-Star 2025 a truly inclusive experience. Historically, multiplayer games had been confined to specific platforms, often leading to divided player bases and frustrating incompatibilities between PC, console, and mobile gamers. All-Star 2025 eliminated these restrictions by introducing universal cross-platform compatibility, allowing players from different devices to compete against one another in real time. The game's advanced networking infrastructure ensured that no player had an unfair advantage, automatically balancing input methods to maintain a level playing field. PC gamers using a mouse and keyboard, console players with controllers, and mobile users with touch controls could all play together without performance disparities affecting competition.

One of the biggest challenges in implementing cross-platform functionality was maintaining fair matchmaking. The development team addressed this by introducing an intelligent matchmaking system that categorized players based on their control method and skill level. This meant that players using similar input methods were paired together, preventing situations where a highly precise mouse-and-keyboard player would be matched against someone using touch controls on a mobile device. Additionally, All-Star 2025 allowed players to switch devices seamlessly without losing progress. A match started on a console could be continued on a tablet or smartphone, thanks to real-time cloud save synchronization.

The impact of cloud gaming and cross-platform play extended beyond just accessibility—it redefined the way communities formed within the game. Players were no longer restricted by platform limitations when teaming up with friends, leading to larger, more dynamic online communities. The ability to play from anywhere, on any device, without compromising performance or quality, made All-Star 2025 a true technological marvel. It marked a new era in gaming where the only requirement to play was an internet connection, breaking down barriers and bringing players together like never before.

Chapter 3
Game Mechanics and Design Innovation

The heart of any great game lies in its mechanics—the intricate system of rules, interactions, and physics that dictate how players engage with the world. While stunning visuals and cutting-edge technology can elevate a gaming experience, it is ultimately the feel of the gameplay that determines its success. All-Star 2025 didn't just aim to follow the best practices of game design; it sought to rewrite the rulebook, introducing innovations that would challenge traditional approaches to competition, immersion, and interactivity. Every movement, action, and decision was carefully crafted to ensure that players felt in control, engaged, and constantly evolving in their skills.

One of the most revolutionary aspects of All-Star 2025's game design was its fluid, physics-based movement system. Traditional first-person and third-person shooters often rely on predefined animations, making movement feel rigid or scripted. In contrast, All-Star 2025 implemented real-time procedural animation, allowing every character action—whether running, dodging, climbing, or engaging in melee combat—to feel natural and dynamic. Players had complete control over their avatar's movements, with seamless transitions between different locomotion states. This resulted in a more organic and immersive gaming experience, where parkour-style movement, wall-running, and momentum-based traversal added a new layer of strategic depth.

Another groundbreaking innovation was the game's adaptive combat system, which went beyond the standard hit-and-shoot mechanics of traditional competitive games. The combat experience in All-Star 2025 was designed to be intuitive yet deeply strategic, incorporating precision-based hitboxes, physics-driven impact calculations, and environment-reactive damage modeling. Whether wielding melee weapons or ranged firearms, players had to consider factors like terrain, weapon weight, and enemy positioning when engaging in combat. No two fights played out the same way, as the game's AI-driven combat physics adjusted dynamically based on player tactics and environmental conditions.

A defining feature of All-Star 2025 was its real-time evolving battlefield mechanics, which introduced destructible environments, shifting terrain, and dynamic weather effects that directly influenced gameplay. Unlike static maps that remained unchanged between matches, All-Star 2025 introduced a living world where player actions left permanent marks. Buildings could collapse under sustained gunfire, walls could be breached to create new pathways, and sudden sandstorms or heavy rain could reduce visibility and force players to rethink their strategies. These dynamic elements ensured that every match felt fresh and unpredictable, pushing players to constantly adapt to their surroundings.

The game also introduced a player-driven progression system, where skills, abilities, and playstyles evolved organically rather than being locked behind rigid upgrade paths. Players could customize their combat abilities, movement techniques, and even the way they interacted with the environment based on their performance and decisions in the game. This level of personalization meant that every player's journey was unique, with no two characters playing exactly the same way.

At its core, the design philosophy behind All-Star 2025 was to reward creativity, adaptability, and skill rather than reliance on pre-programmed mechanics. The game's systems encouraged experimentation, mastery, and strategic thinking, ensuring that players who innovated and evolved would always have an edge. With its blend of physics-driven gameplay, adaptive combat, and player-controlled progression, All-Star 2025 wasn't just a game—it was a new way to experience competitive gaming.

The Evolution of Competitive Play

Competitive gaming has come a long way from its humble beginnings. What started as friendly arcade battles and local LAN tournaments has evolved into a global industry, complete with million-dollar prize pools, professional teams, and millions of spectators watching online and in packed arenas. All-Star 2025 did not just join the ranks of competitive games—it redefined what it meant to compete at the highest level. By introducing groundbreaking mechanics, AI-driven strategy adaptations, and a dynamic playing environment, the game elevated competition to new heights and reshaped the esports landscape.

One of the most significant innovations in All-Star 2025 was its adaptive skill-based matchmaking system, which ensured that players were always challenged at the right level. Unlike older matchmaking models that relied solely on numerical rankings, All-Star 2025 utilized machine learning algorithms to analyze a player's playstyle, strategic choices, and response to in-game events. This meant that instead of simply matching players based on win/loss ratios, the game adjusted matchups based on individual performance trends, making every battle feel engaging and fair. This system rewarded skill development, encouraging players to refine their techniques and learn new strategies rather than relying on repetitive tactics.

Another major advancement was the integration of evolving AI opponents into competitive play. In traditional competitive games, human players dominate the esports scene, but All-Star 2025 introduced AI-driven competitors that could be trained by real players. These AI entities learned from the best human players and could participate in matches, providing a challenge even when human competition was unavailable. Some tournaments even featured hybrid matches, where human players faced off against AI opponents that had been trained by the top-ranked pros, pushing the limits of strategic adaptability.

The game also revolutionized the spectator experience, an essential part of modern competitive gaming. In traditional esports, viewers often had to rely on commentators and fixed camera angles to understand the action. All-Star 2025 introduced interactive live-view technology, which allowed spectators to control their own viewing angles, access real-time statistics, and even jump into virtual reality modes to experience the game from a player's perspective. This level of immersion turned casual viewers into active participants, bridging the gap between players and audiences.

One of the defining features of All-Star 2025's competitive play was its dynamic and destructible environments, which forced players to adapt their strategies on the fly. Unlike static maps in traditional competitive games, All-Star 2025's battlegrounds changed over time. Players could create new pathways, destroy cover, and use environmental hazards to their advantage. This innovation added an extra layer of unpredictability, ensuring that even veteran players had to constantly evolve their tactics rather than memorizing fixed strategies.

Beyond mechanics, All-Star 2025 reshaped the esports ecosystem by allowing cross-platform competitive play. Players on PC, console, and even mobile could enter the same tournaments, with balanced mechanics ensuring fairness across different input methods. This eliminated the historical divide between platforms, uniting players in one truly universal competitive arena.

By combining cutting-edge AI, evolving mechanics, and an immersive spectator experience, All-Star 2025 transformed competitive gaming into a living, breathing battlefield where adaptability and intelligence were just as important as reflexes and mechanical skill. It was not just another esports title—it was a revolution in competitive play, setting a new standard for the future of gaming.

Player-Driven Storytelling

One of the most innovative aspects of All-Star 2025 was its player-driven storytelling, a feature that allowed players to shape the game's narrative in ways never before seen in competitive gaming. While many multiplayer games focus solely on mechanics and competition, All-Star 2025 introduced a living, evolving world where player actions influenced the storyline, game environment, and future updates. Instead of following a static, developer-controlled script, the game's world was shaped by the choices and interactions of its player base, making each experience unique and deeply personal.

At the core of this system was the dynamic narrative engine, which responded to player behaviors, victories, and alliances to create a non-linear story progression. In traditional games, storylines are predetermined, with fixed cutscenes and dialogue paths. However, in All-Star 2025, every match, tournament, and battle played a role in shaping the game's larger story. Events in ranked play, open-world conflicts, and even small-scale community interactions were tracked and integrated into the game's lore, allowing players to influence the world in real-time.

The game's faction-based system played a crucial role in player-driven storytelling. Players could align themselves with different factions, each with its own ideology, goals, and playstyle. The rise and fall of these factions were determined not by developers but by player actions and the outcomes of large-scale battles. If one faction dominated in online matches, it could gain more control over in-game territories, unlocking exclusive missions, resources, and advantages. Conversely, if another faction staged a comeback, the game world would shift accordingly, altering objectives and introducing new plotlines. This real-time evolution of power dynamics made every season of All-Star 2025 feel fresh and unpredictable.

Another major innovation was the interactive lore system, which encouraged players to uncover the game's backstory through exploration and competition. Hidden within the game world were relics, encrypted messages, and environmental storytelling elements that revealed pieces of the game's overarching mystery. Some of these discoveries were locked behind major multiplayer milestones, meaning that the global player base had to work together—or against each other—to unlock the next chapter of the game's unfolding saga. As new pieces of lore were discovered, they were incorporated into in-game events, missions, and even character interactions, creating a constantly evolving narrative landscape.

Perhaps the most ambitious feature of All-Star 2025's storytelling was its community-driven world-building events, where developers allowed players to directly shape the future of the game through high-stakes, limited-time scenarios. In some instances, entire cities in the game's open world were destroyed or rebuilt based on the actions of top-ranking teams. Special tournaments determined the fate of major characters, and collective player choices in seasonal events led to permanent changes in the game's lore. This approach made every player feel like an integral part of the narrative, reinforcing the idea that their actions had lasting consequences.

By combining competitive gameplay with emergent storytelling, All-Star 2025 blurred the line between gaming and narrative-driven experiences. It was no longer just about winning matches—it was about shaping the history of a living, breathing game world, making every player an active participant in a grand, ever-evolving story.

Revolutionary Control Systems

One of the most groundbreaking aspects of All-Star 2025 was its revolutionary control system, which redefined how players interacted with the game world. In traditional competitive gaming, control schemes have often been rigid, with minimal evolution beyond button-mashing mechanics and standardized input layouts. All-Star 2025 broke away from these conventions by introducing an adaptive, intuitive control system that offered players unparalleled precision, flexibility, and immersion. By combining gesture-based inputs, haptic feedback, AI-assisted controls, and cross-device compatibility, the game elevated player control to a level never before seen in competitive gaming.

At the core of the new control system was its fluid movement technology, which allowed players to execute advanced maneuvers with natural ease. Traditional games relied on animation presets for running, dodging, and attacking, often leading to repetitive and predictable character movements. All-Star 2025 introduced real-time procedural animation, meaning that each movement responded dynamically to player input and environmental factors. Whether a player was sprinting through an open battlefield, scaling walls, or dodging an incoming projectile, the game adjusted movement physics in real time to ensure that every action felt smooth and realistic.

A key innovation in the control system was the intelligent input adaptation, which analyzed each player's playstyle and adjusted control responsiveness accordingly. This meant that whether a player used a controller, keyboard and mouse, touchscreen, or a VR motion system, the game provided an optimized experience. AI-driven algorithms adjusted sensitivity, button layouts, and response times to match individual preferences, ensuring that no input method had an unfair advantage. This seamless cross-platform input integration allowed console, PC, and mobile players to compete on an even playing field.

For players using VR and motion-based controls, All-Star 2025 introduced an advanced gesture recognition system. Rather than relying on static button presses, VR players could perform actions using natural hand movements. A flick of the wrist could execute a quick melee attack, while a sweeping motion could activate a defensive maneuver. Haptic feedback gloves enhanced this experience by allowing players to physically "feel" the weight of their weapons, the impact of a hit, or the tension of a drawn bowstring.

This level of realism made combat in All-Star 2025 feel more immersive and responsive than ever before.

Another major advancement was the adaptive combat controls, which changed dynamically based on in-game scenarios. If a player switched from long-range sniping to close-quarters melee combat, the game adjusted the control scheme automatically to enhance precision. Weapon recoil, movement acceleration, and camera sensitivity adapted in real time to match the intensity of the situation. This ensured that combat felt natural and fluid, eliminating the need for players to make constant manual adjustments.

One of the most ambitious features of All-Star 2025's control system was its brain-computer interface (BCI) compatibility, which allowed for mind-controlled inputs. While still in its early stages, this technology enabled players using specialized neural headsets to perform certain in-game actions—such as issuing commands or activating abilities—through brain signals alone. This was a monumental leap in accessibility, providing an innovative way for players with physical disabilities to engage with the game at a competitive level.

By combining real-time procedural animation, intelligent input adaptation, motion-based controls, and even neural integration, All-Star 2025 delivered a revolutionary control experience that reshaped how players interacted with competitive gaming. It was not just about pressing buttons—it was about seamlessly connecting the player's instincts, actions, and strategies with the game world, making every moment feel more responsive, immersive, and empowering.

The Perfect Balance of Strategy and Action

A great competitive game requires more than just fast reflexes or high-speed action—it demands a deep layer of strategy that rewards tactical thinking as much as raw mechanical skill. All-Star 2025 achieved this balance masterfully, blending fast-paced action with thoughtful strategy, ensuring that players had to be both quick on their feet and sharp in their decision-making. By integrating real-time tactical mechanics, adaptive AI-driven gameplay, and a dynamic environment that responded to player choices, All-Star 2025 created a competitive experience where every match was as much a mental challenge as it was a test of physical skill.

One of the key innovations that defined this balance was the situational adaptability system, which ensured that no single playstyle could dominate every match. Players had to adjust their approach based on the ever-changing battlefield, the strengths and weaknesses of their team, and the evolving strategies of their opponents. Unlike traditional shooters or battle arenas where pre-determined metas dictated the best strategies, All-Star 2025 encouraged constant innovation. The game's AI-driven match analytics would assess in-game decisions in real time, adjusting environmental factors, enemy tactics, and available resources to force players into dynamic problem-solving situations.

The real-time strategy integration was another key factor in balancing action with thoughtful play. While All-Star 2025 had the intense firefights and skill-based combat that players expected from a top-tier action game, it also introduced tactical elements that encouraged planning and team coordination. Players could deploy real-time defenses, set traps, disrupt enemy supply lines, and manipulate terrain to gain an advantage. Every action had a consequence—reckless aggression could expose vulnerabilities, while overly defensive play could allow the enemy to control key objectives.

The resource management system added another layer of strategy to gameplay. Unlike traditional games where ammo, health, and abilities were replenished predictably, All-Star 2025 introduced dynamic resource allocation, where players had to manage their equipment carefully. High-powered weapons had limited ammunition, special abilities required strategic energy conservation, and environmental resources could be depleted or controlled by opposing teams. This forced players to make strategic decisions on the fly—whether to conserve resources for a final push, invest in early dominance, or adapt based on the flow of battle.

The AI-driven enemy intelligence system further deepened the strategy-action balance. In both competitive and cooperative play, enemies would adapt dynamically to the player's approach. If a team relied too heavily on long-range attacks, the enemy AI would adjust by closing the distance and forcing close-quarters engagements. If a team coordinated too predictably, the AI would disrupt their strategies with counter-maneuvers. This real-time strategic evolution ensured that every encounter felt fresh, requiring players to rethink their approach constantly.

Lastly, the skill expression system ensured that both strategic depth and raw skill were rewarded equally. While high-level players with exceptional reflexes and accuracy had an advantage in direct combat, smart players who outmaneuvered their opponents, controlled objectives, and executed clever tactics could turn the tide of battle. This meant that All-Star 2025 catered to a wide range of competitive gamers, from fast-paced action players to slow, methodical strategists.

By successfully blending real-time strategy, dynamic adaptability, resource management, and skill-based combat, All-Star

2025 perfected the balance between action and strategy. It created a game where thinking ahead was just as important as reacting fast, ensuring that every match felt unpredictable, rewarding, and endlessly engaging.

Chapter 4
The Rise of the All-Star Community

A great game is not just defined by its mechanics, visuals, or even its success in competitive play—it is defined by its community. All-Star 2025 was more than just a game; it was a movement that brought players together in ways never before seen in the industry. The rise of the All-Star community transformed the game into a cultural phenomenon, creating an ecosystem where players, content creators, developers, and esports professionals all played a role in shaping its future. Through organic engagement, deep social integration, and a thriving fanbase that extended beyond the screen, All-Star 2025 became a shared experience rather than just another title in gaming history.

The game's community-driven approach was evident from the beginning. Unlike traditional games that relied solely on developer-created content, All-Star 2025 gave its players a voice in shaping the game world. With real-time player-influenced storylines, faction-driven conflicts, and seasonal world events dictated by player actions, the community played an active role in how the game evolved over time. This interactive storytelling ensured that no two playthroughs were ever the same, keeping engagement levels high and allowing players to feel personally invested in the game's universe.

Social connectivity was another key element in the rise of the All-Star community. The game was designed to seamlessly integrate with streaming platforms, social media, and content creation tools, allowing players to share their experiences effortlessly. Whether it was a highlight reel of an epic battle, a tutorial on advanced mechanics, or a funny in-game moment, All-Star 2025 encouraged players to become content creators in their own right. Built-in clip-sharing tools, AI-driven replay highlights, and custom game modes allowed the community to generate and distribute content like never before. As a result, the game dominated online discussions, turning casual players into influencers and influencers into game ambassadors.

Esports played a monumental role in fueling the game's competitive ecosystem and community engagement. The All-Star 2025 professional scene took off almost instantly, with major tournaments attracting millions of viewers worldwide. What set this competitive scene apart was its inclusivity and accessibility—players from all platforms could compete in ranked leaderboards, and AI-driven training modules allowed casual players to hone their skills before entering high-level play. The game's spectator tools made it easier than ever for fans to follow their favorite players, analyze plays, and even participate in interactive live events, where viewers could influence in-game elements in real-time.

But perhaps the most remarkable part of the All-Star community was its organic, player-led initiatives. Fans created in-depth wikis, strategy guides, and coaching communities, fostering an environment where new players could quickly learn and improve. Developers actively engaged with the community through regular updates, balancing patches, and player-feedback forums, ensuring that player voices were heard in shaping the game's evolution. This symbiotic relationship between players and developers built a sense of trust and loyalty that few games had achieved before.

Ultimately, All-Star 2025 was more than just a title—it was a social experience that extended beyond the screen. Through deep player involvement, community-driven storytelling, and an esports scene that welcomed everyone, All-Star 2025 didn't just build a fanbase—it built a legacy. The rise of the All-Star community proved that when players are given the tools, voice, and freedom to contribute, they don't just play the game—they become part of its history.

How Fans Shaped the Game

A great game is built by developers, but a legendary game is shaped by its players. All-Star 2025 was not just a developer-driven project; it was a game that evolved through the passion, creativity, and dedication of its fans. Unlike traditional games where updates, expansions, and balance changes were dictated solely by the developers, All-Star 2025 embraced a community-driven approach, allowing players to influence nearly every aspect of the game. From shaping the storyline and game mechanics to creating their own content and driving competitive esports, the fans of All-Star 2025 turned it into more than just a game—they made it a living, breathing universe.

One of the most significant ways fans shaped All-Star 2025 was through player-influenced storylines. Instead of a rigid, pre-written narrative, the game's world evolved based on collective player decisions, in-game events, and major tournament outcomes. Faction wars, seasonal conflicts, and even character arcs were influenced by how the global community played. When one faction gained dominance over another due to player victories, the game's lore adapted to reflect this shift, introducing new missions, territories, and alliances. This real-time evolving story made every season feel like a unique chapter in gaming history, written by the actions of its players.

Fans also had a direct impact on game mechanics and balancing. Unlike many competitive games that require months or even years for developers to respond to player feedback, All-Star 2025 featured community-driven balancing updates. Through integrated feedback systems, polling mechanisms, and live data tracking, developers could quickly assess how new mechanics were affecting gameplay and respond accordingly. Players weren't just consumers of the game—they were active contributors to its refinement. This collaboration ensured that no overpowered strategies dominated for too long and that every update was aligned with the needs of the community.

The modding and user-generated content scene also played a massive role in shaping All-Star 2025. The game provided powerful built-in creation tools that allowed players to design custom maps, game modes, skins, and even entirely new challenges. Some of these fan-made creations became so popular that the developers officially integrated them into the core game, further blurring the line between developer-driven content and community contributions. This level of creative freedom meant that All-Star 2025 never felt stale—players were constantly discovering new experiences crafted by fellow gamers.

Esports and competitive gaming were another area where fans played a crucial role. The professional scene wasn't just driven by major gaming organizations—it was built by grassroots tournaments, community-run leagues, and player-led initiatives. Fans organized their own online competitions, developed in-depth strategy guides, and coached newcomers, creating an ecosystem where anyone could rise through the ranks and become a top-tier competitor. The game's built-in spectator tools and streaming integrations made it easier than ever for community-driven events to gain recognition, further solidifying All-Star 2025 as a player-first esports title.

Beyond the game itself, All-Star 2025's cultural impact was driven by its fanbase. Online communities, forums, social media, and content creation platforms became extensions of the game, where players shared their experiences, theories, and legendary moments. Fan-made cinematics, lore discussions, and viral clips kept the game relevant even outside of play sessions.

Through their creativity, dedication, and engagement, fans didn't just shape All-Star 2025—they defined it. They turned it from a competitive game into a movement, ensuring that every match, every update, and every season carried the mark of the players who made it their own.

The Impact of Streamers and Content Creators

In the modern gaming landscape, success is no longer dictated solely by traditional marketing or developer-driven promotions. Instead, streamers and content creators have become some of the most influential voices in shaping a game's popularity, longevity, and cultural relevance. All-Star 2025 was no exception. Its rise to prominence was fueled not just by its groundbreaking mechanics but by the enthusiastic community of streamers, YouTubers, and social media influencers who turned it into a global phenomenon.

One of the key reasons All-Star 2025 became a favorite among content creators was its highly dynamic and unpredictable gameplay. Unlike many competitive games that rely on pre-set mechanics or scripted moments, All-Star 2025 featured player-driven interactions, evolving strategies, and real-time environmental changes. This meant that no two matches were ever the same, creating endless opportunities for engaging content. Streamers could showcase jaw-dropping plays, analyze high-level strategies, or simply entertain their audiences with unexpected, hilarious in-game moments. The game's built-in replay system allowed for seamless clip-sharing, ensuring that content creation was not only easy but also encouraged as part of the game's experience.

The developers of All-Star 2025 recognized the power of content creators early on and built features specifically to support them. The game included streamer-friendly overlays, interactive audience tools, and real-time analytics, allowing streamers to engage with their viewers in new and innovative ways. Spectator modes enabled audiences to control their own viewing perspectives, and interactive Twitch and YouTube integrations let viewers vote on in-game events, spawn challenges, or even impact the game's weather conditions in special modes. This level of audience participation turned passive viewers into active participants, deepening their connection to both the game and the content creator.

Esports and competitive streaming were another crucial aspect of All-Star 2025's success. With large-scale tournaments, high-stakes ranked matches, and influencer-driven challenge events, the game provided an ideal platform for both professional players and casual streamers to showcase their skills. The integration of live coaching tools and community-led training programs meant that aspiring players could learn from the best, fueling an ongoing cycle of engagement where content creators weren't just entertainers — they were also mentors and analysts.

Beyond Twitch and YouTube, short-form content platforms like TikTok and Instagram Reels played a significant role in All-Star

2025's cultural impact. Thanks to its high-speed action and cinematic visuals, the game lent itself perfectly to bite-sized, viral clips that showcased insane trick shots, last-second victories, or hilarious in-game glitches. These moments spread rapidly across social media, attracting new players who might not have otherwise considered playing a competitive game.

Another important factor in the game's success was developer-streamer collaboration. Unlike traditional gaming companies that operated with a top-down approach, All-Star 2025's developers actively worked with content creators, taking their feedback, integrating player-driven changes, and even designing limited-time modes based on popular trends. This two-way relationship ensured that content creators felt like they had a real stake in the game's evolution, motivating them to continue producing high-quality content and keeping their audiences engaged.

Ultimately, All-Star 2025 thrived because it embraced the new era of gaming entertainment, where players don't just play a game — they experience it through their favorite creators. Streamers and content creators weren't just promoting the game; they were an integral part of its identity, helping to shape its culture, strategies, and community in ways that no traditional marketing campaign ever could.

Building a Global Player Base

The success of All-Star 2025 wasn't just about innovative mechanics, immersive storytelling, or cutting-edge technology — it was about reaching players from every corner of the world and making them feel like part of a unified gaming community. From the start, the developers envisioned a game that would transcend regional barriers, cultural differences, and hardware limitations, creating an ecosystem where players from different countries, backgrounds, and skill levels could connect, compete, and collaborate. Through global accessibility, localized engagement, and a focus on inclusivity, All-Star 2025 built one of the most expansive and diverse player bases in gaming history.

A key factor in the game's worldwide appeal was its cross-platform play and cloud gaming support. By eliminating the need for expensive hardware, All-Star 2025 allowed players to experience the game on high-end gaming PCs, next-generation consoles, mobile devices, and even smart TVs. Cloud gaming technology ensured that even those with limited hardware capabilities could enjoy the game at full graphical fidelity, as all the processing was handled on remote servers. This democratization of access meant that players in developing countries, who might not have had access to top-tier gaming setups, could still compete on an even playing field.

Localization was another crucial aspect of the game's global expansion. Unlike many Western-developed games that struggle to gain traction in non-English-speaking regions, All-Star 2025 was fully localized in over 30 languages, including voiceovers, subtitles, and culturally relevant UI adaptations. The game's marketing campaigns, in-game events, and even character designs were tailored to different regions, ensuring that players from Asia, Europe, the Middle East, South America, and beyond felt equally represented. Special regional servers and time zone-friendly matchmaking ensured that players could engage in competitive play without suffering from high ping or inconvenient scheduling.

Another important element of All-Star 2025's global strategy was community-driven expansion. Instead of relying solely on traditional marketing, the developers leveraged regional influencers, esports teams, and fan-driven initiatives to promote the game in different territories. Streamers from diverse backgrounds were given early access, allowing them to introduce the game to their audiences in a way that felt natural and authentic. Player-driven tournaments, fan art contests, and local meetups helped cement the game's presence in various gaming cultures, from Japan's ultra-competitive esports scene to South America's fast-growing mobile gaming market.

Esports played a massive role in uniting the global player base. Unlike many competitive games that focus primarily on North America and Europe, All-Star 2025 took a truly international approach, ensuring that tournaments were held in multiple regions with fair prize pools and sponsorship opportunities. The game's region-based competitive leagues allowed emerging players from smaller esports markets to rise through the ranks, creating new gaming stars in countries that had previously been overlooked in mainstream competitive gaming.

Inclusivity also played a key role in the game's expansion. All-Star 2025 featured customizable accessibility settings to ensure that players of all abilities could participate. Adaptive control schemes, text-to-speech support, and alternative input methods meant that no one was left behind. Additionally, the game's commitment to diverse representation in character design, narrative arcs, and voice acting helped players see themselves reflected in the game world.

By removing technical barriers, embracing localization, fostering community-driven growth, and championing inclusivity, All-Star 2025 didn't just build a player base—it built a global gaming movement. The game became more than just a competitive battleground; it became a shared space where players from every part of the world could connect, compete, and create lasting memories together.

Esports and Competitive Leagues

Esports has grown from a niche hobby to a billion-dollar industry, with professional gamers achieving celebrity status and global tournaments drawing millions of viewers. All-Star 2025 was built with competitive gaming in mind, ensuring that from the very beginning, it would be a game that defined the next generation of esports. With a structured competitive ecosystem, fair and skill-based matchmaking, and multi-tiered leagues that catered to both casual and professional players, All-Star 2025 revolutionized the way esports functioned, making high-level play more accessible, engaging, and rewarding than ever before.

A key feature of All-Star 2025's esports success was its intelligent matchmaking and ranking system. Unlike traditional competitive games that solely relied on win/loss ratios to determine rank, All-Star 2025 introduced performance-based ranking using AI-driven analytics. This system considered factors like player decision-making, teamwork, accuracy, reaction time, and adaptability, ensuring that true skill was rewarded rather than just grinding out wins. This approach prevented issues like "smurfing" (high-level players dominating lower ranks) and made climbing the leaderboards feel genuinely meaningful.

The game also introduced a multi-tiered league structure, allowing players of all skill levels to engage with competitive play at different intensities. The Amateur Leagues provided casual competitors with an entry point to structured gameplay, where they could compete for in-game rewards, recognition, and local bragging rights. The Semi-Pro Circuits were designed for serious players looking to make a name for themselves, featuring regional tournaments, community-hosted events, and online qualifiers that acted as a stepping stone to professional play. The Global Pro League (GPL) was the pinnacle of competition, featuring franchise-based teams, million-dollar prize pools, and high-production live events that were streamed worldwide.

One of the most groundbreaking innovations of All-Star 2025's esports scene was the cross-platform competitive format. While many traditional esports games kept PC, console, and mobile players separate, All-Star 2025 leveled the playing field by balancing mechanics and refining input-based matchmaking. This allowed players across different platforms to compete together fairly, expanding the reach of esports and making tournaments more inclusive. The game's use of adaptive AI training partners further helped bridge the gap, allowing players to practice against AI opponents modeled after real esports pros, preparing them for high-level competition.

The broadcast experience for esports was also transformed in All-Star 2025, making it one of the most viewer-friendly competitive games ever made. Unlike traditional static camera views, All-Star 2025 introduced interactive spectator modes, allowing viewers to switch between player perspectives, access real-time statistics, and even use VR technology to "step into" the matches as virtual spectators. These innovations made watching All-Star 2025 tournaments an immersive and engaging experience, bringing fans closer to the action than ever before.

Beyond structured leagues, All-Star 2025 also embraced community-driven tournaments, allowing grassroots organizers and local gaming communities to host their own competitions with in-game tools for matchmaking, sponsorships, and prize distribution. This support for independent organizers ensured that esports was not just for professionals but for players at every level, helping the competitive scene grow organically from the ground up.

By combining intelligent ranking systems, inclusive tournament structures, immersive spectator experiences, and AI-driven training tools, All-Star 2025 built an esports ecosystem that was as competitive as it was accessible. Whether you were a casual player, a rising talent, or an elite professional, the game provided a pathway to greatness, ensuring that competitive gaming was no longer limited to a privileged few but open to anyone with the skill and dedication to succeed.

Chapter 5
The Cultural Phenomenon

A game is not just measured by its mechanics, graphics, or sales figures—it is measured by the impact it leaves on culture, society, and the way people interact with entertainment. All-Star 2025 was more than just a best-selling title or an esports sensation; it became a global cultural phenomenon, influencing everything from fashion and music to social media trends and even education. It was not just a game people played—it was a game that defined an era.

From the moment of its launch, All-Star 2025 captured the imagination of millions, becoming a staple of internet culture and mainstream entertainment. Unlike past competitive games that remained confined to gaming circles, All-Star 2025 broke through into music, television, films, and even global brand collaborations. Its characters became pop culture icons, its in-game terminology was adopted into everyday slang, and its competitive matches were broadcast alongside traditional sports events.

One of the most significant aspects of All-Star 2025's cultural impact was its role in shaping digital identity and self-expression. The game offered unparalleled customization options, allowing players to create characters that truly reflected their personalities, interests, and cultures. From fashion-forward skins designed in collaboration with real-world brands to emotes and gestures inspired by trending dances, All-Star 2025 became a virtual playground where identity and creativity flourished. For many players, their in-game avatars became extensions of themselves, making the game as much a social platform as it was a competitive experience.

Social media played a crucial role in All-Star 2025's rise as a cultural touchstone. Viral gameplay moments, hilarious in-game glitches, and record-breaking tournament highlights spread across platforms like TikTok, Twitter, Instagram, and YouTube, creating a constant buzz that kept the game in public conversation. Memes, reaction videos, and fan-generated content transformed All-Star 2025 into more than just a pastime—it became an integral part of digital culture, with millions engaging with the game even if they didn't play it themselves.

Music and entertainment were also deeply influenced by the game. All-Star 2025 featured soundtracks composed by top-tier artists, and exclusive in-game concerts allowed musicians to premiere their latest songs in a fully immersive, interactive environment. These digital music festivals blurred the line between gaming and live entertainment, attracting not just hardcore gamers but also fans of global pop culture. The game's impact was so profound that fashion brands, sportswear companies, and even high-end designers partnered with the game to launch exclusive virtual apparel, bridging the gap between gaming and mainstream fashion.

Beyond entertainment, All-Star 2025 influenced education, technology, and even business innovation. Schools and universities began using the game's simulation and strategic gameplay for training in teamwork, leadership, and problem-solving. Tech companies studied its AI-driven mechanics and cloud gaming infrastructure to advance developments in other industries, while businesses recognized the power of All-Star 2025-style engagement in marketing, branding, and interactive advertising.

By becoming a cultural movement rather than just a game, All-Star 2025 achieved something few titles ever had—it became a defining feature of modern digital life, shaping the way people played, interacted, expressed themselves, and even saw the future of entertainment.

The Game That Defined a Generation

Every era in gaming history has had its defining moments—titles that pushed boundaries, shaped communities, and left an undeniable mark on popular culture. All-Star 2025 was not just another successful game; it was a movement, a technological breakthrough, and a cultural phenomenon that defined an entire generation of gamers. It wasn't merely played—it was experienced, lived, and integrated into the everyday lives of millions around the world. From its revolutionary mechanics to its impact on esports, entertainment, and social interaction, All-Star 2025 changed the way people engaged with digital worlds.

One of the defining aspects of All-Star 2025 was its ability to bring people together like never before. Gaming had always been a social activity, but All-Star 2025 elevated this interaction into something more immersive and meaningful. Its cross-platform play and cloud gaming accessibility allowed players from all over the world, regardless of their hardware, to participate in the same competitive universe. Whether playing on a high-end PC, a console, or a mobile device, players could compete on equal footing, breaking down barriers that had long divided gaming communities.

The game's impact extended far beyond its core gameplay. It revolutionized esports, creating a competitive ecosystem that was inclusive, engaging, and constantly evolving. Unlike previous titles where esports was an exclusive space dominated by a few elite players, All-Star 2025 introduced AI-driven training tools, community-driven leagues, and interactive spectator experiences, allowing more people to participate in and enjoy competitive gaming. It wasn't just the professionals who defined All-Star 2025—the everyday player had just as much influence on shaping its legacy.

Beyond competition, All-Star 2025 transformed how gaming was viewed in mainstream culture. It blurred the line between gaming and other entertainment industries, with in-game concerts featuring global artists, virtual fashion collaborations, and even digital storytelling experiences that evolved based on player choices. It wasn't uncommon to see references to All-Star 2025 in movies, music videos, and social media, proving that the game had become more than a pastime—it had become a cultural touchstone.

Social media played a crucial role in cementing All-Star 2025's place as a generational icon. Viral moments from the game—whether an epic comeback in a tournament, a hilarious in-game glitch, or a perfectly executed team strategy—became trending topics worldwide. TikTok, YouTube, and Twitch were flooded with content, making All-Star 2025 a household name even among those who didn't play it. Its memes, catchphrases, and player-driven narratives became ingrained in everyday conversations, further proving its deep cultural penetration.

Perhaps the most important reason All-Star 2025 defined a generation was its ability to evolve with its players. Unlike static games that remained unchanged after release, All-Star 2025 was a living, breathing world that adapted based on community input. Its dynamic storylines, balance updates, and user-generated content ensured that the game remained fresh, relevant, and exciting, no matter how many years passed.

A game that defines a generation is not just one that sells millions of copies—it is one that leaves a lasting legacy. All-Star 2025 did exactly that. It shaped the way people viewed gaming, competition, and online interaction. It wasn't just the game of the year; it was the game of an era—a title that future generations would look back on as a turning point in gaming history.

The Influence on Pop Culture

Few games have had the ability to transcend the gaming world and embed themselves into mainstream pop culture. All-Star 2025 was not just a competitive multiplayer experience; it became a cultural movement, influencing music, fashion, film, social media, and even the way people interact with technology. The game's characters, aesthetics, and community-driven elements found their way into everyday life, proving that All-Star 2025 was more than just a game—it was a global phenomenon that shaped the entertainment industry.

One of the clearest signs of All-Star 2025's cultural dominance was its impact on fashion and brand collaborations. The game introduced highly customizable character skins and outfits, many of which were created in partnership with real-world fashion brands, sportswear companies, and luxury designers. These virtual outfits became so popular that some designs were turned into real-world clothing collections, allowing fans to wear their in-game aesthetic in everyday life. Streetwear brands launched exclusive All-Star 2025-themed apparel, and even high-fashion labels collaborated with the game, proving that gaming had firmly established itself in the world of style and personal expression.

Music was another industry that saw a massive influence from All-Star 2025. The game's dynamic soundtrack featured original compositions from top artists, as well as in-game concerts and interactive music events that blurred the line between gaming and live entertainment. Musicians from different genres, including hip-hop, electronic, and rock, contributed exclusive songs to the game, and some even premiered new albums within the virtual world. These concerts attracted millions of live viewers, making All-Star 2025 one of the most innovative platforms for music distribution and fan engagement.

Social media played a crucial role in amplifying the game's cultural reach. Viral TikTok trends, reaction videos, and gameplay challenges kept All-Star 2025 constantly trending, even among those who weren't hardcore gamers. Dance emotes from the game became popular in real-life dance challenges, and meme-worthy moments from the game spread rapidly across platforms like Twitter, Instagram, and YouTube. Unlike previous games that relied on traditional marketing, All-Star 2025 thrived on organic community engagement, ensuring its presence in everyday conversations and digital spaces.

Hollywood and the entertainment industry also embraced All-Star 2025. Television shows, movies, and web series began referencing the game, whether through character easter eggs, storyline tie-ins, or direct collaborations. Some films even integrated All-Star 2025 mechanics and visual styles into their action sequences, further solidifying its place in mainstream entertainment. The game's rich lore and cinematic storytelling led to the development of animated series, comic books, and digital spin-offs, allowing its universe to expand beyond the confines of the game itself.

Perhaps the most profound impact All-Star 2025 had on pop culture was its role in redefining digital identity and social interaction. The game provided a space where players could express themselves, build relationships, and engage in meaningful storytelling. Its fusion of competitive gaming, creative customization, and social connectivity made it more than just entertainment—it became a lifestyle.

By seamlessly integrating with mainstream culture, All-Star 2025 proved that gaming was no longer a subculture—it was a dominant force in shaping modern entertainment, fashion, music, and digital interaction. Its influence reached far beyond the screen, making it one of the most culturally significant games of its generation.

Fashion, Music, and Entertainment Crossovers

In the modern entertainment industry, video games are no longer isolated experiences—they have become integral to global pop culture, merging with fashion, music, and film in ways that were once unimaginable. All-Star 2025 took this concept to another level, seamlessly blending gaming with mainstream entertainment and creating a multi-dimensional experience that extended far beyond the digital battlefield. Through strategic brand collaborations, in-game concerts, and cinematic tie-ins, All-Star 2025 transformed from a game into a cultural hub, where fashion icons, music superstars, and Hollywood filmmakers all found a place to showcase their creativity.

One of the game's most significant contributions to pop culture was its fashion collaborations. The extensive customization options allowed players to create unique avatars, and soon, real-world fashion brands took notice. Luxury labels, streetwear brands, and sports apparel companies began launching limited-edition in-game skins, allowing players to dress their characters in high-end designer outfits that reflected real-world fashion trends. Some of these collaborations even crossed over into real life, with physical clothing lines inspired by in-game cosmetics. High-profile brands like Nike, Adidas, Gucci, and Off-White created All-Star 2025-themed collections, proving that gaming was no longer separate from the fashion industry—it was a major player within it.

Music also played a crucial role in All-Star 2025's rise as a cultural phenomenon. The game's dynamic soundtrack featured tracks from top-charting artists, and its in-game music festivals became must-attend digital events. Unlike traditional music releases, where fans listen to new songs passively, All-Star 2025 gave them an interactive way to experience music. Global superstars hosted in-game concerts, where players could explore virtual festival grounds, engage in synchronized dance emotes, and participate in exclusive live music events. These interactive concerts attracted millions of viewers, bridging the gap between gaming and the music industry in a way that had never been done before. Musicians used the game as a platform to debut new songs, albums, and even entire visual experiences, proving that virtual worlds were the future of live entertainment.

The entertainment industry also embraced All-Star 2025, leading to crossovers with Hollywood films, TV series, and animated productions. Major blockbuster franchises collaborated with the game, releasing exclusive in-game character skins, special mission tie-ins, and limited-time story arcs that directly connected with upcoming movie releases. Some characters from All-Star 2025 even made appearances in mainstream media, comics, and animated series, expanding the game's lore into other entertainment formats.

One of the most groundbreaking innovations was the introduction of cinematic storytelling within the game, where seasonal events featured high-quality cutscenes directed by renowned filmmakers. This approach blurred the lines between gaming and film, turning All-Star 2025 into a storytelling platform that evolved over time based on player actions. With the rise of virtual influencers and digital celebrities, All-Star 2025 characters became cultural icons, recognized beyond the gaming community and embraced by mainstream audiences.

By integrating fashion, music, and entertainment seamlessly into its universe, All-Star 2025 redefined what a game could be. It was no longer just an interactive experience—it was a platform for artistic collaboration, cultural expression, and global entertainment, proving that the future of pop culture was interactive, immersive, and deeply connected to gaming.

Memes, Trends, and the Internet Effect

In the digital age, a game's success is no longer measured solely by sales numbers or critical reviews—it's also about how deeply it permeates internet culture. All-Star 2025 became more than just a game; it was a social phenomenon fueled by memes, viral trends, and constant engagement on social media platforms. Through organic community-driven content, hilarious gameplay moments, and cultural crossovers, All-Star 2025 didn't just dominate the gaming industry—it became a defining feature of internet culture, shaping the way people interacted with games, humor, and entertainment.

One of the biggest factors behind the game's internet dominance was its meme-worthy gameplay moments. With its dynamic physics engine, unexpected interactions, and sometimes chaotic battle sequences, All-Star 2025 naturally generated hilarious, unpredictable moments that players rushed to share. Whether it was an impossible trick shot, a perfectly timed glitch, or a player using an unconventional strategy to win a match, these clips spread rapidly across TikTok, Twitter, Instagram, and Reddit, fueling endless discussions and keeping the game relevant in everyday online conversations.

The developers understood the power of viral content and embraced it fully. Unlike traditional game studios that might try to suppress glitches or overly "goofy" mechanics, the team behind All-Star 2025 actively leaned into them, adding in-game emotes, animations, and even special event modes inspired by viral trends. If a meme or joke gained traction in the community, it often found its way into the game in some form—whether as a playable gesture, a limited-time game mechanic, or an Easter egg hidden within the game world. This level of responsiveness to player-driven humor built a stronger connection between developers and the community, making fans feel like they were part of the creative process.

One of the game's most significant internet impacts was on TikTok and YouTube Shorts, where short-form content creators capitalized on the game's fast-paced action and engaging visual style. Entire trends were built around All-Star 2025, from dance emotes that became real-world viral sensations to reaction videos of players pulling off near-impossible stunts. Challenges like "No Weapon Wins" or "Only Parkour Battles" became community-wide phenomena, inspiring even non-gamers to engage with the content.

Beyond gameplay, the game's characters, catchphrases, and visual aesthetics became widely recognized in meme culture. Fans created remixes, parody edits, and animated skits that spread across the internet, further cementing All-Star 2025 as a cultural mainstay. Some of the game's voice lines and sound effects were even sampled in popular music tracks, movie trailers, and reaction videos, proving that its influence extended beyond gaming.

Perhaps the most fascinating part of All-Star 2025's internet effect was its ability to unite different online communities. Unlike games that appeal to a niche audience, All-Star 2025 was embraced by competitive gamers, casual players, streamers, artists, and even non-gaming content creators, making it one of the most widely discussed and shared games in online history.

By becoming a living part of internet culture, All-Star 2025 proved that modern gaming success isn't just about gameplay—it's about how a game resonates with people, sparks creativity, and becomes embedded in the way we communicate online. It was more than a game; it was an internet movement that reshaped gaming's role in digital entertainment.

Chapter 6
The Business of Gaming

The gaming industry has evolved from a niche entertainment sector into one of the most lucrative and influential industries in the world, surpassing film and music in revenue. At the heart of this transformation is a new approach to game development, distribution, and monetization—one that prioritizes engagement, accessibility, and long-term profitability over traditional single-purchase models. All-Star 2025 didn't just succeed as a game; it redefined the business of gaming, setting new standards for revenue generation, brand partnerships, and player-driven economies. Its success highlighted how modern games are no longer just products but platforms that generate sustained engagement and financial growth.

One of the most important shifts in the gaming industry, and a key reason for All-Star 2025's success, was the free-to-play model combined with smart monetization strategies. Instead of relying solely on upfront sales, the game implemented a live-service business model, where the base game was free, but revenue came from in-game purchases, battle passes, cosmetic skins, and seasonal events. This approach lowered the barrier to entry, allowing millions of players to experience the game without financial commitment while ensuring a steady flow of revenue from those who chose to invest in additional content.

A major factor in the game's financial success was its player-driven economy. All-Star 2025 introduced an in-game marketplace where players could buy, sell, and trade digital assets, including skins, weapons, and unique character items. Limited-edition cosmetic items, designed in collaboration with fashion brands, sports organizations, and movie studios, became highly sought-after, turning virtual goods into a multi-million-dollar marketplace. Some exclusive skins and collectibles even held real-world value, with rare items selling for thousands of dollars on secondary markets, much like digital art in the NFT space.

Brand partnerships also played a crucial role in monetization. Unlike traditional product placements in video games, All-Star 2025 seamlessly integrated global brands into its universe, making collaborations feel natural rather than forced. Major companies launched themed in-game items, promotional challenges, and interactive brand experiences, creating a new advertising model where players actively engaged with brands rather than passively consuming ads. This model became a blueprint for the future of advertising in gaming, showing that immersive brand integration could be both profitable and player-friendly.

Esports and streaming also fueled the game's economic ecosystem. All-Star 2025 tournaments generated massive sponsorship deals, ticket sales, and media rights agreements, making the competitive scene a significant revenue stream. Streaming platforms like Twitch and YouTube saw record-breaking viewership during major in-game events, attracting advertisers eager to reach gaming audiences. This reinforced gaming as not just an entertainment medium but a mainstream spectator sport with real economic power.

By leveraging a free-to-play model, live-service updates, player-driven economies, brand collaborations, and esports monetization, All-Star 2025 showcased the new frontier of gaming business models. It proved that games were no longer just one-time purchases but long-term platforms capable of generating billions in revenue while keeping players engaged for years. The business of gaming had changed, and All-Star 2025 was at the forefront of this revolution.

The Multi-Billion Dollar Success

The success of All-Star 2025 wasn't just measured in player numbers or cultural impact—it was a financial juggernaut, reshaping how games were monetized and proving that interactive entertainment was one of the most powerful economic forces in the world. Within just a few years, All-Star 2025 surpassed expectations, generating billions in revenue and solidifying its place among the most profitable games of all time. Through a combination of strategic monetization, esports expansion, brand partnerships, and player-driven economies, the game became a financial powerhouse that set new benchmarks for the industry.

One of the key reasons for All-Star 2025's staggering success was its free-to-play model with high engagement-based monetization. By removing the traditional upfront purchase barrier, the game attracted millions of players worldwide. Instead of making money through a one-time sale, the developers implemented a live-service revenue model, relying on seasonal battle passes, cosmetic skins, exclusive digital items, and in-game events. This approach ensured that revenue flowed continuously, as players willingly spent money on customization options, character upgrades, and exclusive rewards that enhanced their experience.

The in-game marketplace and player-driven economy became another major source of financial success. Unlike previous games where cosmetic items had fixed prices, All-Star 2025 introduced a dynamic trading system, where players could buy, sell, and trade rare skins, weapons, and collectibles. This created a thriving digital economy, where some limited-edition items became valuable assets, fetching thousands of dollars on secondary markets. Digital collectibles, some released in collaboration with real-world brands and fashion designers, turned into status symbols within the game's community, driving up demand and making virtual goods as desirable as physical ones.

Esports was another massive revenue driver, elevating All-Star 2025 beyond just a game and into the realm of professional competition. With multi-million dollar tournaments, global leagues, and sponsorship deals with major brands, the game revolutionized competitive gaming as a business. Streaming platforms like Twitch, YouTube, and TikTok saw record-breaking viewership, leading to lucrative broadcast rights deals, merchandise sales, and ticketed live events. Brands flocked to sponsor teams, events, and even individual players, further integrating gaming into mainstream sports culture.

The game's collaborations with Hollywood, music, and global brands added another layer to its financial success. Unlike traditional advertising, where companies paid for product placements, All-Star 2025 flipped the model—brands paid to be featured in the game. Fashion houses launched limited-time digital outfits, movie studios introduced exclusive themed events, and musicians premiered new albums through in-game concerts, generating revenue from both in-game purchases and cross-promotion deals.

By combining free-to-play accessibility, continuous content updates, esports expansion, brand partnerships, and player-driven digital economies, All-Star 2025 created a multi-billion dollar ecosystem that redefined how video games were monetized. It was no longer just a best-selling game—it was an economic giant, proving that interactive entertainment wasn't just competing with traditional media but leading the future of global entertainment revenue.

Marketing Strategies That Worked

The commercial success of All-Star 2025 wasn't just the result of an engaging game—it was the outcome of one of the most innovative, data-driven, and community-focused marketing strategies in gaming history. Unlike traditional game launches that relied on large advertising budgets and conventional promotions, All-Star 2025 leveraged a multi-layered marketing approach that combined organic engagement, influencer collaborations, viral social media trends, and experiential events. These strategies didn't just sell the game—they made players feel like they were part of something bigger, turning All-Star 2025 into a cultural phenomenon.

One of the most groundbreaking marketing tactics was the use of in-game marketing events and teasers. Rather than relying on trailers or commercials, the developers introduced in-game narrative teasers, special events, and mystery challenges that gradually built hype for major content updates. Players discovered cryptic messages, easter eggs, and interactive countdowns embedded within the game itself, encouraging speculation and engagement across social media platforms. This approach turned marketing into an interactive experience, making players feel like they were uncovering secrets rather than being marketed to.

The game's strategic use of influencers and content creators played a pivotal role in its success. Instead of focusing solely on traditional gaming influencers, All-Star 2025 partnered with streamers, musicians, athletes, and even fashion icons, ensuring that the game appealed to multiple demographics. Content creators were given exclusive early access, behind-the-scenes insights, and customizable in-game items, allowing them to promote the game authentically to their audiences. This grassroots approach built trust and credibility, making the game feel like a community-driven movement rather than a corporate product.

One of the most effective marketing strategies was social media engagement and viral challenges. All-Star 2025 wasn't just advertised on platforms like TikTok, Twitter, Instagram, and YouTube—it became an integral part of trending conversations, memes, and gaming culture. The developers actively encouraged players to participate in viral gameplay challenges, dance emote trends, and content-sharing contests, turning everyday players into brand ambassadors. Some of the most successful campaigns saw players competing in creative challenges—from no-weapon survival runs to elaborate in-game trick shots—leading to millions of user-generated videos that promoted the game organically.

Another innovative approach was real-world brand partnerships and experiential marketing. The game launched exclusive collaborations with major brands, offering limited-edition merchandise, in-game skins inspired by real-world fashion, and even pop-up gaming events in major cities. Live events featured interactive demos, celebrity showdowns, and AR-powered installations, creating buzz across social media. The seamless integration of gaming with mainstream culture helped attract non-traditional gamers, expanding the player base beyond the competitive gaming community.

Finally, All-Star 2025 capitalized on seasonal content drops and FOMO (fear of missing out) marketing. The game introduced limited-time skins, battle passes, and rotating event-exclusive content, encouraging players to stay engaged and return frequently. Time-limited collaborations with popular franchises, music artists, and esports teams created a sense of urgency, driving both player retention and in-game purchases.

By combining immersive storytelling, influencer partnerships, social media-driven engagement, experiential branding, and FOMO-based monetization, All-Star 2025 executed a marketing campaign that didn't just promote a game—it built a lasting, engaged community. This strategy didn't just sell copies; it cemented All-Star 2025 as a cultural icon that players wanted to be part of, both in-game and in real life.

In-Game Monetization and Ethics

As the gaming industry evolved, so did the strategies for monetization. All-Star 2025 was at the forefront of this shift, generating billions in revenue through a combination of in-game purchases, battle passes, digital economies, and brand collaborations. However, unlike many games that faced criticism for aggressive monetization tactics, All-Star 2025 took a player-friendly, ethical approach that balanced profitability with fairness, transparency, and long-term engagement. The game became a model for how developers could generate sustainable revenue without exploiting players.

One of the key pillars of All-Star 2025's monetization strategy was its free-to-play model, which allowed anyone to download and play the game without an upfront cost. This lowered the barrier to entry, making the game accessible to millions. Instead of relying on pay-to-win mechanics or forcing players into microtransactions, All-Star 2025 focused on cosmetic-based monetization, ensuring that paid items did not provide competitive advantages. Players could purchase skins, emotes, weapon designs, and unique character animations, but the core gameplay remained balanced for all users, regardless of spending habits.

A major ethical concern in modern gaming is loot boxes and gambling mechanics. Many games have faced backlash for using randomized rewards that encourage excessive spending, especially among younger players. All-Star 2025 avoided predatory loot boxes and instead introduced a transparent, direct-purchase system. Players knew exactly what they were buying, removing the gambling element from in-game purchases. For those who enjoyed the thrill of unlocking rewards, the game offered battle passes and achievement-based progression systems, allowing players to earn exclusive content by playing rather than paying.

Another standout feature was the game's player-driven economy, which introduced a fair trading system for in-game items. Unlike traditional monetization models where developers controlled all transactions, All-Star 2025 allowed players to trade, sell, and collect digital assets, creating a thriving in-game marketplace. This approach empowered the community by letting them assign value to rare items, ensuring that players who invested time into the game could reap rewards without feeling forced to spend real money.

The developers also prioritized ethical pricing and regional affordability. Recognizing that gaming is a global industry with diverse economic conditions, All-Star 2025 implemented regional pricing models, ensuring that digital purchases remained fair across different countries. Instead of adopting a one-size-fits-all approach, the game adjusted prices based on local purchasing power, making it more accessible to players in emerging gaming markets.

Perhaps one of the most innovative ethical monetization features was "Play to Give" initiatives, where a portion of in-game revenue from special charity-themed events was donated to global causes. Players could purchase exclusive skins, banners, and in-game items while knowing their money was going toward environmental efforts, mental health support, and gaming accessibility programs. This approach built trust with the player base, proving that monetization could be both profitable and socially responsible.

By balancing player-first monetization, ethical design principles, and long-term sustainability, All-Star 2025 demonstrated that gaming businesses could thrive without resorting to exploitative tactics. The game's approach set a new industry standard, proving that profitability and player respect can coexist, creating a model for future live-service games to follow.

The Future of Gaming Business Models

The gaming industry is undergoing a rapid transformation, moving beyond traditional one-time purchases to more dynamic, long-term business models. As technology evolves and player expectations shift, developers are finding new ways to monetize games while ensuring accessibility, engagement, and ethical practices. All-Star 2025 was at the forefront of this shift, proving that the future of gaming lies in sustainable, player-friendly monetization models that prioritize community involvement, digital economies, and immersive experiences.

One of the most significant changes in gaming business models is the dominance of live-service games and subscription-based monetization. Instead of selling standalone titles, developers are increasingly adopting games-as-a-service (GaaS) models, where continuous updates, expansions, and seasonal content keep players engaged over time. All-Star 2025 thrived under this system, introducing seasonal battle passes, rotating in-game events, and evolving storylines that encouraged long-term investment. This approach is likely to become the industry standard, as it allows developers to generate ongoing revenue while delivering fresh content that keeps players engaged for years.

Subscription services are also shaping the future of gaming. Platforms like Xbox Game Pass, PlayStation Plus, and cloud gaming services have proven that players are willing to pay for access rather than individual game ownership. This model ensures steady revenue for developers while lowering the entry cost for players. The next evolution of this model could be cross-game subscription ecosystems, where multiple studios collaborate to offer a shared library of live-service titles, further expanding accessibility.

Another major innovation in gaming business models is the rise of player-driven economies and digital asset ownership. All-Star 2025 introduced a thriving in-game marketplace where players could buy, sell, and trade rare cosmetic items, character skins, and collectibles. The success of these digital economies suggests that future games will lean heavily into player-to-player trading and blockchain-backed digital ownership, allowing gamers to truly own and trade virtual goods across different platforms. This could lead to the emergence of cross-game economies, where assets from one game hold value in another, creating a metaverse-like ecosystem of connected virtual worlds.

The integration of branded collaborations and experiential marketing is also shaping future gaming business models. Instead of traditional advertising, brands are now paying to be integrated directly into the game world, offering in-game clothing, virtual concerts, and themed events. All-Star 2025 set the blueprint for this approach, proving that games are not just entertainment—they are social hubs where brands can engage with a digital-native audience. As augmented reality (AR) and virtual reality (VR) expand, the gaming industry will likely see even more interactive brand experiences, where digital and physical worlds blend seamlessly.

Ethical monetization will also play a crucial role in the future of gaming business models. Players are increasingly aware of predatory microtransactions, pay-to-win mechanics, and gambling-based loot boxes, pushing developers to adopt more transparent, player-first monetization strategies. Future business models will likely favor direct purchases, fair trade systems, and content-based progression, ensuring that players feel rewarded rather than exploited.

Ultimately, the future of gaming business models is about flexibility, accessibility, and sustainability. As technology continues to evolve, developers will need to strike a balance between profitability and player satisfaction, ensuring that games remain immersive, rewarding, and financially viable for both companies and players alike. The gaming industry is no longer just about selling games—it's about building long-term digital experiences that shape the future of entertainment itself.

Chapter 7
The Controversies and Challenges

No game reaches the heights of All-Star 2025 without facing its share of controversies and challenges. As one of the most successful and culturally impactful games of its era, All-Star 2025 also found itself at the center of heated debates, community backlash, and industry-wide discussions. While it revolutionized competitive gaming, esports, and monetization models, it also had to navigate the challenges of balancing player satisfaction, ethical concerns, and the evolving landscape of gaming regulations.

One of the earliest controversies surrounding All-Star 2025 was its monetization strategy, particularly the introduction of premium cosmetic skins and battle passes. While the game avoided predatory loot boxes and pay-to-win mechanics, some players criticized the high prices of limited-time skins and event-exclusive content, arguing that the game encouraged FOMO-based spending (fear of missing out). The debate over whether All-Star 2025 was fair in its monetization practices or simply exploiting its massive player base sparked discussions about ethical game design and the fine line between profitability and player respect.

Another major challenge was game balance and competitive fairness. With millions of players worldwide and an ever-evolving meta, maintaining a balanced gameplay experience became increasingly difficult. Certain weapons, abilities, and characters were often deemed overpowered, leading to frequent demands for nerfs and reworks. The developers had to walk a fine line between keeping the game fresh with new content while ensuring that no single strategy dominated competitive play. Some updates that sought to rebalance the game were met with outrage from the community, as players who had invested time mastering certain mechanics suddenly found them weakened or removed altogether.

The rise of cheating and hacking in All-Star 2025 was another major issue that threatened the integrity of the game. As with any highly competitive title, the presence of aimbots, wallhacks, and third-party cheating software led to frustration among legitimate players. While the developers implemented AI-driven anti-cheat systems and strict account bans, the battle against cheaters became a constant struggle. Some competitive tournaments were even compromised by cheating scandals, leading to investigations and heated debates about how gaming companies should handle cheating in online multiplayer games.

The game also faced censorship and regional regulatory challenges in certain markets. In some countries, concerns over violent content, microtransactions, and data privacy led to restrictions, modifications, or outright bans of the game. The developers had to navigate cultural sensitivities, government policies, and legal challenges to ensure the game remained accessible globally while complying with regional laws. This highlighted the ongoing tension between gaming as a global industry and the diverse legal and cultural standards of different nations.

Perhaps the most unexpected controversy came from within the community itself. Toxicity in online gaming has long been an issue, and All-Star 2025 was no exception. Despite robust moderation tools,

AI-powered reporting systems, and community guidelines, the game struggled with harassment, in-game toxicity, and esports player misconduct scandals. While the developers took a proactive stance against these issues, the ongoing challenge of creating a welcoming and respectful gaming environment remained a point of contention.

Despite these challenges, All-Star 2025 demonstrated resilience and adaptability, addressing controversies head-on and working to refine its approach in response to player feedback. These issues weren't just obstacles—they were growing pains in the evolution of modern gaming, forcing the industry to confront important ethical, legal, and social questions about the future of interactive entertainment.

Balancing Innovation with Player Expectations

One of the greatest challenges faced by any game that reaches the scale of All-Star 2025 is maintaining a balance between innovation and player expectations. While constant updates, new mechanics, and fresh content are essential to keeping a game relevant, too much change—or the wrong kind of change—can alienate long-time players. Striking the right balance between pushing the boundaries of game design while respecting the preferences of the community is one of the hardest yet most crucial aspects of modern game development.

From the start, All-Star 2025 positioned itself as a game-changer in competitive gaming, introducing cutting-edge technologies like AI-powered NPCs, real-time physics-driven combat, and evolving player-driven storylines. These innovations made the game stand out, but they also meant that players had to constantly adapt to new mechanics, meta shifts, and evolving strategies. While many embraced the challenge, others expressed frustration when updates altered gameplay elements they had spent months mastering. This led to a recurring debate: how much innovation is too much?

One of the primary sources of contention was game balance and competitive fairness. Every time the developers introduced a new weapon, ability, or game mode, it had the potential to disrupt the existing meta. Some players felt that frequent adjustments to character abilities and weapon stats forced them to relearn strategies too often, while others appreciated the constant evolution that kept the game from feeling stagnant. The challenge for the developers was ensuring that innovation didn't undermine competitive integrity, leading to a delicate cycle of player feedback, balance patches, and data-driven adjustments.

Another key issue was the tension between casual and hardcore players. As All-Star 2025 grew, its player base became increasingly diverse, ranging from casual gamers who played for fun to professional esports competitors who relied on the game for their careers. Some updates catered to one group at the expense of the other—for example, simplifying mechanics to make the game more accessible sometimes frustrated veteran players who had invested significant time mastering its complexities. The developers had to carefully balance accessibility with depth, ensuring that the game remained welcoming to newcomers while still offering enough depth for skilled players to continue improving.

The introduction of AI-driven opponents and evolving NPC behaviors was another controversial point. While some players loved the realism and unpredictability that AI added to the game, others felt that AI-controlled elements took away from the core player-vs-player (PvP) experience. The developers had to carefully integrate these AI systems so that they enhanced, rather than replaced, the competitive spirit that defined All-Star 2025.

Perhaps the biggest lesson learned from balancing innovation with player expectations was the importance of communication and transparency. Every time a major update was introduced, the developers made sure to engage with the community through live developer Q&As, patch notes, and beta testing feedback loops. This ensured that players felt heard and involved in the evolution of the game, reducing backlash while fostering trust.

In the end, the key to balancing innovation with player expectations wasn't about avoiding change—it was about introducing change thoughtfully and collaboratively. All-Star 2025 showed that the future of game development isn't just about pushing technology forward—it's about keeping players engaged, respected, and part of the creative process.

Addressing Toxicity in the Community

No online game is immune to toxicity, and All-Star 2025 was no exception. With millions of players worldwide, the game fostered an incredible sense of community, but it also faced challenges related to harassment, cheating, player misconduct, and negative in-game behavior. As online gaming grew in popularity, so did concerns about how competitive environments could breed cyberbullying, discrimination, and unsportsmanlike behavior. Recognizing the importance of creating a safe, welcoming, and respectful environment, the developers of All-Star 2025 implemented proactive solutions to address toxicity, enforce fair play, and cultivate a positive gaming culture.

One of the first steps in tackling toxicity was developing an advanced, AI-driven moderation system. Traditional reporting mechanisms often relied on manual review, leading to delayed responses and inconsistent punishments. To counter this, All-Star 2025 introduced a real-time AI moderation system that could detect abusive language, harassment, and unsportsmanlike conduct through chat analysis, voice recognition, and behavioral tracking. Players who engaged in hate speech, threats, or disruptive behavior received automatic warnings, temporary mutes, or account suspensions, depending on the severity of their actions. This system ensured swift enforcement of community guidelines, making it clear that toxic behavior would not be tolerated.

A major innovation in player accountability was the introduction of the Reputation System. Unlike traditional matchmaking that focused solely on skill level, All-Star 2025 incorporated player behavior into matchmaking rankings. Players with a history of positive interactions, teamwork, and fair play were rewarded with faster queue times and exclusive in-game rewards, while those with multiple reports for toxicity, griefing, or rage-quitting were placed in restricted matchmaking pools with others who displayed similar behavior. This approach incentivized good sportsmanship while keeping toxic players separate from the general community.

To further combat negativity, the game introduced enhanced reporting and feedback tools. Players could report toxic behavior with a single click, and the system provided detailed feedback when actions were taken. If a reported player received a ban or warning, the reporter was notified, reinforcing trust in the moderation system. Additionally, a community-driven tribunal system allowed veteran players with high reputation scores to review flagged content, helping to ensure fair and balanced enforcement.

Esports and professional gaming were not exempt from toxicity, and All-Star 2025 took a firm stance on player conduct in tournaments and live-streamed events. Competitive players and influencers were held to strict codes of conduct, with penalties for engaging in harassment, cheating, or promoting toxic behavior. High-profile bans and suspensions sent a clear message that no player, regardless of their skill or fame, was above the rules.

Perhaps the most important initiative was fostering a culture of positivity and inclusivity. The game featured built-in communication guidelines, player mentorship programs, and AI-driven encouragement tools, which promoted constructive feedback instead of hostility. Players who demonstrated outstanding teamwork, leadership, and sportsmanship were rewarded with special titles, badges, and in-game currency, reinforcing positive behavior.

Through a combination of AI-driven moderation, reputation-based matchmaking, community enforcement, and proactive developer engagement, All-Star 2025 set a new standard for addressing toxicity in gaming. By making respect and fairness a core part of the player experience, the game proved that competitive gaming could be intense and engaging without being toxic.

Microtransactions and Pay-to-Win Debates

As gaming evolved, so did its business models, with microtransactions becoming a core component of modern monetization strategies. While microtransactions have allowed games to be more accessible by offering free-to-play experiences, they have also sparked ongoing debates about fairness, pay-to-win mechanics, and ethical monetization practices. All-Star 2025, despite its massive success, was not exempt from these discussions. While the game implemented cosmetic-based microtransactions rather than pay-to-win mechanics, there were still controversies, player concerns, and industry-wide conversations about how monetization affects competition and player enjoyment.

From the start, All-Star 2025 adopted a free-to-play model with in-game purchases, allowing players to access the game without any upfront cost. This model removed the financial barrier to entry, ensuring that players from different economic backgrounds could participate. However, to sustain its profitability, the game introduced a variety of purchasable digital items, including skins, emotes, weapon designs, and limited-time event cosmetics. The developers emphasized that these items were purely cosmetic and did not provide any gameplay advantages, making it clear that skill—not spending—determined success in the game.

Despite this cosmetic-only approach, the game still faced pay-to-win accusations, particularly regarding exclusive event items and battle pass rewards. Some players argued that while the game did not sell power directly, certain skins, animations, or effects provided psychological advantages in competitive play. For example, some high-tier skins had subtle visual effects that made them harder to detect in certain environments, or specific character animations were perceived as having smoother movement patterns. These concerns led to discussions about whether visual customization should be regulated to ensure a completely level playing field.

Another controversial topic was the pricing of microtransactions. Some premium skins were priced at higher-than-expected rates, leading to community backlash about affordability and exclusivity. While developers defended these prices by emphasizing that they were optional and did not affect gameplay, critics argued that limited-time exclusive items created a "FOMO" (Fear of Missing Out) effect, pressuring players into spending money to secure rare cosmetics. To address these concerns, All-Star 2025 later introduced grindable in-game currency, allowing dedicated players to earn premium items without spending real money, which helped ease frustrations around exclusivity.

Perhaps the biggest debate surrounding microtransactions was the use of battle passes and loot mechanics. While All-Star 2025 avoided traditional loot boxes, which have been widely criticized for their resemblance to gambling, the battle pass system was structured in a way that required consistent gameplay to unlock high-tier rewards. Some players felt that this system pressured them into spending more time than they otherwise would just to justify the purchase of the pass. Others saw it as a fair exchange, providing rewards for engagement rather than random luck.

To maintain player trust, the developers committed to transparency and ethical monetization, regularly engaging with the community through feedback surveys, pricing adjustments, and alternative earning methods. They also implemented regional pricing adjustments, ensuring that digital purchases remained fair and accessible across different countries.

Ultimately, All-Star 2025 demonstrated how microtransactions could be successful without resorting to pay-to-win mechanics. However, the ongoing debates about fairness, exclusivity, and accessibility highlighted the complex relationship between monetization and player satisfaction, proving that the future of in-game purchases must balance profitability with ethical design.

The Role of Government Regulations

As the gaming industry continues to expand, government regulations have become an essential factor in shaping the way developers design, market, and monetize their games. The rise of microtransactions, loot boxes, data privacy concerns, and esports gambling has led to increased scrutiny from policymakers worldwide. All-Star 2025, as one of the most commercially successful and culturally influential games of its era, found itself at the center of numerous regulatory debates, facing legal challenges, regional restrictions, and compliance requirements across different countries. The game's journey highlighted the growing intersection between gaming, law, and consumer protection, forcing the industry to navigate an evolving legal landscape.

One of the most controversial aspects of gaming regulations is loot boxes and gambling mechanics. Many governments have classified loot boxes as a form of predatory gambling, especially when they involve randomized rewards that players can purchase with real money. While All-Star 2025 avoided direct loot box mechanics, some of its monetization strategies—such as limited-time event skins and battle pass progression systems—still drew regulatory attention. Countries like Belgium, the Netherlands, and South Korea imposed strict rules on randomized digital purchases, forcing the developers to modify certain in-game transactions in specific regions to comply with local laws.

Another significant area of regulation was data privacy and consumer protection. As All-Star 2025 operated on a cloud-based infrastructure with AI-driven matchmaking and behavioral tracking, concerns arose regarding how player data was collected, stored, and used. The European Union's General Data Protection Regulation (GDPR), along with similar laws in California (CCPA) and China (PIPL), required the developers to implement transparency policies, secure data encryption, and allow players to manage their personal data preferences. These compliance measures ensured that user information remained protected, preventing potential exploitation or misuse of player data for marketing or algorithmic manipulation.

The impact of gaming on minors also became a focal point of regulation. Governments worldwide debated whether games like All-Star 2025 should include stricter parental controls, spending limits, and age restrictions. Some regions introduced legal requirements for companies to implement spending caps for young players, while others mandated enhanced parental control tools, such as real-time playtime monitoring, spending alerts, and opt-in features for digital purchases. These regulations reflected broader concerns about gaming addiction, psychological manipulation, and the ethical implications of monetization models targeting younger audiences.

Esports also became a regulatory battleground, particularly in areas related to player contracts, prize money taxation, and competitive fairness. As All-Star 2025 grew into a global esports phenomenon, governments began intervening in contract negotiations, labor rights, and fair compensation for professional players. Some countries required that esports teams provide health benefits, retirement plans, and standardized contracts, treating esports athletes with the same legal protections as traditional sports professionals.

Despite these challenges, government regulations also played a positive role in improving industry standards. Regulations forced developers to adopt ethical monetization practices, enhance security protections, and create a safer gaming environment. By embracing compliance and adapting to legal frameworks, All-Star 2025 demonstrated that successful gaming companies can thrive while prioritizing ethical business practices, consumer rights, and long-term sustainability. As the industry continues to grow, government intervention will remain a key factor in shaping the future of interactive entertainment.

Chapter 8
Behind the Scenes – The Developers' Journey

Behind every groundbreaking game lies a team of visionaries, developers, artists, and designers who pour their creativity, technical expertise, and passion into making it a reality. All-Star 2025 was no exception. While the game became a global phenomenon, its development process was a journey filled with innovation, challenges, setbacks, and triumphs. From its initial concept to the final product that captivated millions, the story of its creation reflects the complexity, ambition, and dedication required to build a truly revolutionary gaming experience.

The development of All-Star 2025 began with a bold vision: to create a game that combined cutting-edge technology, competitive depth, and immersive storytelling into one seamless experience. The developers wanted to push the boundaries of what was possible in multiplayer gaming, incorporating features like real-time physics-based combat, AI-powered NPCs, and a player-driven storyline. This level of ambition required years of research, experimentation, and technological breakthroughs to bring to life.

One of the biggest challenges during development was creating a game engine that could handle the game's ambitious scope. While many studios rely on existing engines, the development team at All-Star 2025 decided to build a customized version of Unreal Engine, optimized for dynamic environmental destruction, real-time physics interactions, and scalable cloud-based multiplayer. This decision significantly delayed early production but ultimately allowed the game to achieve unparalleled fluidity and realism in movement, combat, and world interactions.

Another major hurdle was balancing game mechanics and competitive fairness. With a global player base spanning casual gamers, esports professionals, and content creators, the team had to ensure that no single playstyle dominated. Early internal playtests revealed unintended exploits, overpowered abilities, and balance-breaking mechanics, forcing developers to iterate and refine gameplay systems continuously. The process of community-driven testing and direct player feedback played a vital role in shaping the final balance of the game, proving that collaborating with players during development leads to better long-term success.

The game's success was also a testament to the creative minds behind its art, animation, and storytelling. The team worked tirelessly to craft a visually stunning world, with detailed character models, dynamic lighting effects, and an evolving environment that reacted to player actions. The narrative team faced the unique challenge of designing a non-linear, player-influenced storyline, where player choices would impact game events, faction conflicts, and in-game lore. Achieving this level of interactivity required an advanced AI-driven narrative engine, allowing the story to evolve dynamically based on global player actions.

However, the journey was not without its difficulties. The team experienced tight deadlines, internal disagreements on creative direction, and immense pressure to meet player expectations. Crunch culture—a common issue in the gaming industry—was something the developers actively worked to avoid, implementing flexible work schedules, remote development options, and mental health initiatives to support their team. This approach ultimately helped retain top talent and maintain creative momentum throughout the game's development cycle.

The story of All-Star 2025's development is not just one of technical achievement and artistic innovation—it is a testament to the passion, dedication, and resilience of the people behind it. Their journey pushed the boundaries of game development, proving that with bold ideas, teamwork, and an unwavering commitment to quality, it is possible to create a game that defines a generation.

The Long Nights and Hard Decisions

Developing All-Star 2025 was not just about creativity and innovation—it was a grueling test of endurance, problem-solving, and sheer determination. While players experienced the polished final product, the road to completion was filled with late nights, difficult choices, and high-pressure situations that tested the limits of the development team. From major technical setbacks to creative disagreements, every breakthrough came at the cost of long hours, unexpected obstacles, and the challenge of balancing ambition with reality.

One of the biggest hurdles was the game's ambitious scope. From the beginning, the developers wanted All-Star 2025 to be more than just another competitive multiplayer game. They envisioned a living, breathing world with evolving player-driven storylines, real-time physics interactions, and AI-driven characters that could adapt dynamically. However, pushing these boundaries meant venturing into uncharted territory, where technical solutions were not readily available. Many nights were spent rewriting code, testing new physics models, and debugging systems that had never been attempted in a live multiplayer setting before.

One of the hardest decisions came during the second year of development, when the team realized that their original game engine would not support their vision. They had initially planned to use an existing engine, but as the complexity of the game grew, it became clear that they needed a customized engine with better scalability, destruction physics, and AI integration. Switching engines mid-development was a massive risk—it required months of rework, increased costs, and a delay in production schedules. However, the decision ultimately paid off, allowing the game to achieve the seamless, high-performance gameplay that players would later experience.

Balancing gameplay mechanics and competitive fairness was another grueling challenge. The team knew that All-Star 2025 had to appeal to both casual gamers and professional esports players, but satisfying both audiences proved to be a delicate balancing act. Early playtests revealed that certain mechanics—such as AI-assisted movement prediction and terrain destruction—gave some players an unfair advantage, leading to heated internal debates on whether to keep or modify these features. Removing them meant losing some of the innovation that set the game apart, but keeping them risked alienating players who wanted a pure skill-based experience. After countless meetings, test sessions, and community feedback reviews, they found a middle ground, refining the mechanics without compromising the game's competitive integrity.

The hardest moments, however, came not from technical hurdles but from the emotional toll of game development. With tight deadlines, industry pressure, and the growing expectations of millions of players, developers often worked 14-hour days, sacrificing personal time, sleep, and social lives to meet milestones. Crunch culture has long been an issue in the gaming industry, and the leadership team at All-Star 2025 worked hard to minimize burnout by offering flexible schedules and mental health support. However, even with these measures, the sheer weight of responsibility and passion for the project kept many developers working far beyond normal hours.

Despite the exhaustion, the team remained driven by the belief that they were creating something truly special. Each challenge they faced, every difficult decision they made, and all the long nights spent perfecting the game led to the creation of a masterpiece that would define a generation. All-Star 2025 was not just a game—it was the result of sacrifice, perseverance, and the unshakable commitment of its creators.

Overcoming Development Roadblocks

Developing a game as ambitious as All-Star 2025 was never going to be smooth sailing. With cutting-edge technology, real-time physics, AI-powered interactions, and a player-driven storyline, the game was destined to face unprecedented technical, creative, and logistical challenges. While the final product seemed seamless to players, the journey to launch was marked by unexpected roadblocks that required quick thinking, adaptability, and sometimes, difficult sacrifices. Overcoming these hurdles was what ultimately shaped the game into the masterpiece it became.

One of the earliest and most complex challenges was ensuring that All-Star 2025 could handle millions of concurrent players without performance issues. The team aimed to create a massive, living multiplayer experience with destructible environments, adaptive AI, and seamless cross-platform play. However, initial tests revealed severe latency issues, frame rate drops, and unexpected crashes when too many players interacted in dynamic environments. To fix this, the developers redesigned their network architecture, optimized data processing, and implemented cloud-based infrastructure to distribute computing power more efficiently. This shift meant delaying certain milestones, but it ensured that the game would be stable at launch, rather than risking a disastrous day-one experience.

Another major roadblock came with the implementation of real-time physics and environmental destruction. The developers wanted a world where everything reacted realistically to player actions—from bullets splintering walls to buildings collapsing based on structural damage. However, in a multiplayer setting, syncing these physics calculations across thousands of players in real time without causing lag was a technical nightmare. After months of unsuccessful testing, the team considered scrapping the feature altogether, fearing that it would compromise performance. However, an alternative approach was discovered: procedural damage modeling, where destruction was pre-calculated by AI to determine realistic breakpoints before being rendered in real time. This allowed players to experience fully destructible environments without overloading the game's servers.

Balancing game mechanics and AI difficulty was another challenge that required significant iteration. The developers had designed AI-powered NPCs that could learn from player behavior, adapting strategies based on past encounters. While this was an exciting innovation, it led to unexpected problems during testing—some AI opponents became too advanced, reacting with inhuman precision and exploiting weaknesses in player strategies, making the game frustratingly difficult. To fix this, the developers implemented behavioral dampening, which limited the AI's learning speed while still allowing it to feel responsive and intelligent without being unfairly difficult.

Perhaps one of the most difficult roadblocks wasn't technical, but internal disagreements about creative direction. Some designers wanted All-Star 2025 to focus purely on esports competition, while others believed the game's narrative elements and open-world features were what set it apart. These creative differences led to intense debates, with some team members fearing that compromises would dilute the game's identity. In the end, the solution was player choice—the game was designed with multiple modes, allowing competitive players to focus on ranked matches while casual players could explore the game's evolving world and story.

Despite these challenges, the developers' commitment to innovation and problem-solving ensured that All-Star 2025 not only survived these roadblocks but emerged stronger. The delays, difficult decisions, and late-night debugging sessions all contributed to a game that would go on to define the future of competitive multiplayer gaming.

The Passion That Drove the Team

Every great game is built on a foundation of technical skill, creativity, and innovation, but the true driving force behind All-Star 2025 was passion. From the first concept sketches to the final moments before launch, the developers poured their hearts, energy, and determination into making a game that would not only entertain but define a generation. Despite the challenges, setbacks, and intense pressure, what kept the team going was a shared love for gaming, a belief in their vision, and an unshakable commitment to pushing the industry forward.

From the start, the team behind All-Star 2025 wasn't just a group of employees working on a project—they were gamers first, developers second. Many had grown up playing the legendary competitive games of past generations, and they knew exactly what made a multiplayer experience feel alive, rewarding, and endlessly replayable. They didn't want to just create another battle arena or esports title; they wanted to elevate the genre by combining fast-paced competitive mechanics with deep player-driven storytelling and cutting-edge technology.

One of the things that set All-Star 2025 apart was the intense attention to detail from every department. The art team wasn't satisfied with just creating visually appealing character skins—they obsessed over how the light reflected off armor, how fabrics moved realistically in different weather conditions, and how every character's design told a story. The audio team meticulously recorded every footstep, weapon reload, and environmental sound to create an immersive soundscape that responded dynamically to the player's movements.

For the game designers, the goal was to make every moment of gameplay feel intuitive yet deeply skill-based. They spent countless hours studying player psychology, movement fluidity, and combat balance, making sure that each action in the game felt smooth, responsive, and rewarding. Every mechanic, from wall-running to advanced counterplay techniques, was refined through thousands of playtests, driven by a desire to make All-Star 2025 one of the most satisfying competitive games ever created.

Even in the toughest moments—when development roadblocks seemed insurmountable or when certain features had to be cut due to time constraints—the team's passion never wavered. They fought through sleepless nights, last-minute redesigns, and external pressures, always believing that the final product would be worth it. Leadership made it a priority to keep morale high, ensuring that developers felt heard, valued, and supported. Unlike many studios that succumbed to crunch culture, the All-Star 2025 team maintained a work environment fueled by collaboration, respect, and shared excitement.

What truly made All-Star 2025 special was the connection between the developers and the players. The team wasn't just building a game—they were building a community, one that they wanted to be a part of themselves. They engaged with fans, listened to feedback, and constantly iterated to make sure that the game stayed true to its vision while evolving alongside its audience.

In the end, All-Star 2025 wasn't just a commercial success—it was a passion project that became a legacy. It proved that when a team is driven by love for their craft and a desire to innovate, they can create something that does more than just entertain—it inspires, unites, and defines a generation.

What Developers Wish Gamers Knew

The relationship between game developers and players is one of the most unique dynamics in the entertainment industry. Unlike movies or books, where audiences passively consume content, video games are interactive experiences that rely on player engagement, feedback, and skill to bring them to life. While gamers are passionate about their favorite titles, there's often a disconnect between what players expect and what goes on behind the scenes. Developing a game—especially one as complex as All-Star 2025—is an intense, time-consuming process, filled with challenges that players don't always see. If developers had one wish, it would be for gamers to understand the effort, sacrifices, and love that go into making the games they play.

One of the biggest misconceptions players have is that game development is easy, and every problem should have a quick fix. Many times, when bugs, balance issues, or technical glitches appear in a game, players assume that fixing them should be as simple as flipping a switch. In reality, game development is a delicate balance of code, design, animation, and server management, where even a small change can cause unintended consequences. A single bug fix can require weeks of testing to ensure it doesn't break other mechanics, making the process far more complex than it appears.

Another thing developers wish gamers knew is that not all creative decisions are made solely for profit. While monetization strategies like battle passes, in-game purchases, and premium skins are common in modern gaming, they are often necessary to keep a live-service game running long-term. Many players assume that every microtransaction is just a cash grab, but in reality, revenue from cosmetics, expansions, and in-game purchases often funds server maintenance, ongoing content updates, and employee salaries. Without sustainable monetization, many games—especially free-to-play ones—would not be able to survive or evolve over time.

Game balancing is another area where players often underestimate the complexity of developer decisions. When a weapon, ability, or character is nerfed, players frequently assume that developers are intentionally ruining the experience or favoring certain playstyles. In truth, balance adjustments are data-driven, based on millions of matches, player feedback, and competitive statistics. Every tweak requires careful consideration to ensure that no single strategy dominates while still keeping the game fun for everyone. The reality is that some changes will always upset a portion of the player base, but they are made with the goal of long-term game health in mind.

Another important thing developers want gamers to understand is that crunch culture and overwork are real issues in the industry. While most developers are passionate about their work, they are still people who have families, personal lives, and limits to how much they can push themselves. When players demand faster updates, more frequent patches, or immediate fixes, they don't always realize the pressure this puts on developers. Many studios work hard to avoid burnout and ensure fair working conditions, but the demand for constant content updates can make it difficult to maintain a healthy balance.

Lastly, developers wish gamers understood how much love and effort they put into every game they create. Most developers are gamers themselves, and they genuinely want to create something fun, memorable, and innovative. Even when things go wrong, their goal is never to frustrate or disappoint players—they are working tirelessly to bring their vision to life while making sure the experience remains enjoyable for the community.

If there's one takeaway, it's this: Developers and gamers are on the same side. Both want games to be exciting, engaging, and rewarding. By fostering mutual respect, patience, and understanding, players and developers can work together to make gaming better for everyone.

Chapter 9
The Competitive Scene – Esports in 2025

The world of esports in 2025 has evolved into a multi-billion-dollar industry, shaping the way people view gaming as both an entertainment spectacle and a legitimate profession. No longer confined to small, niche tournaments, competitive gaming now rivals traditional sports, with massive global audiences, high-stakes prize pools, and dedicated esports infrastructures that rival major league organizations. In this thriving landscape, All-Star 2025 emerged as one of the defining titles of the era, blurring the lines between traditional competition, digital entertainment, and interactive media.

As the competitive gaming industry matured, it moved beyond simple tournaments and streaming platforms, integrating with mainstream sports, sponsorship deals, and live entertainment events. The biggest esports organizations no longer just represented teams; they became brands with global influence, securing deals with companies that once focused solely on traditional sports sponsorships. The rise of stadium-sized gaming events, interactive fan participation, and cross-platform accessibility meant that esports were no longer just watched—they were experienced.

In this dynamic ecosystem, All-Star 2025 found itself at the forefront of the esports revolution. The game's fast-paced mechanics, high skill ceiling, and deep strategic elements made it a perfect fit for competitive play. With a well-balanced ranking system, tournament-ready infrastructure, and AI-assisted coaching features, All-Star 2025 allowed players to progress from casual play to professional competition seamlessly. Unlike older esports titles, where breaking into the pro scene required extensive networking and external sponsorships, All-Star 2025 integrated path-to-pro mechanics within the game itself, giving every talented player a shot at success.

One of the most innovative aspects of esports in 2025 was the interactive nature of tournaments. Fans no longer just watched—they participated. Esports broadcasting evolved beyond simple livestreams into immersive, interactive events, where audiences could influence aspects of the game in real-time, vote on tournament maps, and even engage in virtual reality spectator modes. This shift redefined esports engagement, making it feel more like a collaborative entertainment experience rather than just a competition.

Cross-platform compatibility also played a significant role in the expansion of competitive gaming. Unlike the past, where esports were dominated by PC and console players, All-Star 2025 embraced mobile and cloud-based gaming, ensuring that players from different platforms could compete on an equal playing field. Cloud gaming's advancements allowed high-end competition to be accessible even in regions where expensive gaming rigs were not common, expanding the talent pool globally and making esports truly international.

Another major shift in 2025 was the integration of AI coaching and analytics into esports training. Gone were the days when teams relied solely on human coaches to break down gameplay footage. Now, AI-assisted systems provided real-time data on player performance, reaction times, tactical positioning, and predictive decision-making. These tools not only enhanced training efficiency but also helped underdog teams rise through the ranks by providing elite-level strategic insights without the need for expensive coaching staff.

With All-Star 2025 leading the way, esports in 2025 became a full-scale digital entertainment industry, where gaming, media, and technology merged to create the next generation of competitive entertainment. The rise of immersive esports experiences, AI-driven competition, and global accessibility ensured that gaming was no longer just a hobby—it was a career, a sport, and a worldwide cultural movement.

The Birth of a New Esports Era

By 2025, esports had evolved into a dominant force in global entertainment, surpassing traditional sports in viewership, engagement, and revenue. What was once a niche competitive scene had transformed into a fully integrated digital sport, complete with structured leagues, multimillion-dollar prize pools, corporate sponsorships, and a dedicated global fanbase. This shift marked the birth of a new esports era, where gaming was no longer just a pastime—it was a career, a business, and a mainstream cultural movement. At the heart of this evolution was All-Star 2025, a game that pushed the boundaries of competitive gaming and played a pivotal role in reshaping the industry.

Unlike previous generations, where esports competitions were largely PC and console-based, the new era of esports embraced cross-platform accessibility. All-Star 2025 was designed to be played on PC, next-gen consoles, mobile devices, and cloud-based platforms, ensuring that anyone, anywhere, could compete at the highest levels. This democratization of esports removed traditional hardware barriers, allowing players from emerging gaming regions to rise through the ranks and compete on a global stage. No longer was esports confined to those with expensive gaming setups—if you had the skills, you had a shot at success.

One of the defining features of this new esports era was the integration of AI-driven analytics and training systems. Esports organizations and independent players alike had access to machine-learning-based coaching tools that could analyze gameplay patterns, optimize strategies, and suggest real-time improvements. AI-assisted coaching became a game-changer, leveling the playing field and giving even lesser-known teams the opportunity to compete with well-established organizations. The introduction of real-time AI-driven in-game commentators also enhanced the viewing experience, allowing audiences to understand the strategy and decision-making process of top-tier players like never before.

Perhaps the most significant change in esports was the evolution of how tournaments were broadcast and experienced. Traditional livestreams had given way to fully interactive esports events, where viewers could switch between player perspectives, participate in live voting, and even influence in-game elements during exhibition matches. Virtual reality (VR) and augmented reality (AR) integration allowed fans to step into the game as spectators, watching matches from the perspective of players or hovering over battlefields in real time. This level of engagement and immersion redefined esports, making it a true spectator sport for the digital age.

The rise of global esports leagues also marked a key shift in this new era. Instead of being limited to regional competitions, All-Star 2025 introduced franchise-based international leagues, where teams from different continents competed in a structured season format, similar to traditional sports leagues. These leagues were backed by major sponsors, broadcasting deals, and partnerships with mainstream sports networks, making competitive gaming as financially viable as professional basketball or soccer.

At the core of this new era of esports was community-driven innovation. Unlike older esports models that were dominated by corporate interests, All-Star 2025 and other modern competitive games placed players, streamers, and fans at the center of their ecosystem. Grassroots tournaments, fan-created content, and player-led initiatives played a significant role in shaping the future of competitive gaming, ensuring that esports remained a community-first experience rather than just a commercial enterprise.

With All-Star 2025 leading the way, the new era of esports had officially begun—one where gaming wasn't just entertainment, but a global movement, an industry powerhouse, and the future of competitive sports.

The Rise of Star Players

As esports continued to evolve into a global spectacle in 2025, a new class of star players emerged, transforming competitive gaming into a stage for individual talent, personality, and influence. Unlike the early days of esports, where teams overshadowed individual recognition, the modern era placed professional gamers on the same pedestal as traditional sports superstars, complete with sponsorship deals, media coverage, and massive fan followings. All-Star 2025 played a pivotal role in this shift, providing a competitive environment where skill, strategy, and personal branding converged to elevate players into global icons.

One of the major factors behind the rise of star players was the increased accessibility and visibility of esports talent. With tournaments being broadcast across Twitch, YouTube, TikTok Live, and even mainstream television networks, millions of viewers tuned in to watch high-stakes matches, insane highlight plays, and dramatic underdog stories unfold in real time. Thanks to advanced player tracking and AI-powered analytics, fans could now follow their favorite competitors like never before, accessing live stats, heat maps, reaction times, and decision-making patterns. This allowed audiences to appreciate the nuances of skill, game sense, and adaptability that set elite players apart.

Social media also played a crucial role in turning top players into celebrities. Unlike past generations of esports professionals who were only recognized within gaming communities, 2025's star players cultivated massive personal brands on platforms like Instagram, TikTok, and Twitter, engaging directly with fans through behind-the-scenes content, training clips, and even personal lifestyle vlogs. This shift not only made esports stars more relatable and accessible but also helped attract new audiences who may not have previously followed competitive gaming.

One defining characteristic of All-Star 2025's competitive scene was the diversity of its star players. The game's cross-platform accessibility allowed for a wider range of talent to rise, breaking down the traditional dominance of PC and console players. Some of the most celebrated competitors came from mobile gaming backgrounds, proving that reflexes, decision-making, and raw talent transcended hardware limitations. Additionally, as the industry became more globalized, players from previously underrepresented regions found themselves competing—and winning—on the biggest stages, shifting the traditional power balance in esports.

The financial and commercial success of these players also changed dramatically. With multimillion-dollar sponsorship deals, exclusive merchandise lines, and even personal NFTs (non-fungible tokens) of in-game achievements, the top-tier professionals in All-Star 2025 enjoyed financial stability comparable to mainstream athletes. Many partnered with brands, endorsing gaming peripherals, energy drinks, clothing lines, and even personal training courses designed to help aspiring gamers improve their skills.

Beyond skill, charisma and personality became just as crucial as in-game performance. Some players gained immense popularity not just for their competitive success, but for their humor, leadership, or inspiring stories of perseverance. Whether it was a former amateur who climbed the ranks through sheer dedication, a strategic mastermind revolutionizing the meta, or a showman who entertained audiences with flashy plays and witty commentary, All-Star 2025 proved that esports stardom was about more than just winning—it was about connection, character, and the ability to captivate a global audience.

In the new era of esports, the rise of star players solidified gaming as a legitimate profession, a media empire, and a global entertainment industry where individual talent could shine as brightly as any traditional sports superstar.

The Biggest Tournaments and Prize Pools

By 2025, esports had fully cemented itself as a global sporting phenomenon, with tournaments that rivaled traditional sporting events in terms of viewership, production value, and financial stakes. What once started as small LAN competitions had evolved into stadium-filling spectacles, where millions of dollars were on the line, and the best players in the world battled for ultimate supremacy. All-Star 2025 played a pivotal role in shaping this new era of high-stakes competitive gaming, hosting some of the biggest tournaments with record-breaking prize pools that redefined what it meant to be an esports professional.

One of the most prestigious tournaments in All-Star 2025 was the All-Star Global Championship (AGC), an annual competition that brought together the best teams and solo players from every continent. The AGC was more than just a tournament—it was a spectacle of entertainment, technology, and high-level gameplay, featuring state-of-the-art augmented reality broadcasts, interactive fan experiences, and real-time audience engagement through VR viewing modes. The prize pool for AGC 2025 exceeded $50 million, making it one of the richest esports tournaments in history, surpassing some of the most well-known traditional sports competitions.

The All-Star Pro League (APL) also played a significant role in All-Star 2025's competitive scene. Unlike traditional one-off tournaments, the APL functioned as a franchise-based league, similar to the NBA or the English Premier League, where teams competed in a structured season format, with sponsorship deals, player salaries, and regional divisions. The league attracted major sports organizations, billion-dollar brands, and celebrity investors, further blending the world of esports with mainstream entertainment. With a combined prize pool of over $100 million spread across the season, the APL provided financial stability and career longevity for professional players, ensuring that gaming was no longer just a hobby—it was a full-fledged professional sport.

Beyond these premier competitions, All-Star 2025 introduced mid-tier and grassroots tournaments with lucrative prize pools, ensuring that rising talents had opportunities to break into the professional scene. Events like the Rising Stars Cup and the

Challenger Series awarded millions in prize money while providing up-and-coming players with visibility, sponsorship opportunities, and potential recruitment into top-tier teams. This tiered tournament structure allowed players from different backgrounds and skill levels to climb their way into the highest levels of competition, making esports more inclusive and accessible than ever before.

Sponsorships and broadcasting rights also played a significant role in increasing prize pools. Major corporations, luxury brands, and tech companies invested heavily in All-Star 2025 tournaments, recognizing the potential of reaching a younger, digitally connected audience. Traditional TV networks fought for broadcast rights, while streaming giants like Twitch, YouTube Gaming, and TikTok Live offered exclusive streaming deals, ensuring that the biggest tournaments reached millions of viewers worldwide.

The rise of crowdfunded prize pools also allowed the community to directly contribute to tournament rewards. Through in-game purchases, battle pass sales, and exclusive tournament skins, players could support their favorite teams and help push prize pools to new heights. This community-driven approach strengthened the connection between esports professionals and their fans, making tournaments feel more collaborative and exciting.

With All-Star 2025 leading the charge, esports in 2025 had become a financial powerhouse, proving that competitive gaming was not just an emerging industry but one of the most lucrative and widely celebrated global sports of the modern era.

The Future of Esports and Competitive Play

Esports has rapidly evolved from a niche subculture into one of the most lucrative and influential industries in global entertainment. As technology advances, competitive gaming is set to become even more immersive, accessible, and financially rewarding, fundamentally changing how players, fans, and organizations engage with the scene. With games like All-Star 2025 leading the way, the future of esports and competitive play promises bigger tournaments, cutting-edge technology, and new ways for players to compete on a global scale.

One of the most significant changes in the future of esports is cross-platform and cloud-based competition. Unlike past decades, where esports was largely limited to PC and console gaming, new advancements in cloud gaming and mobile technology have made high-level competitive play available to anyone with a stable internet connection. All-Star 2025 pioneered seamless cross-platform integration, allowing players on PC, consoles, and mobile devices to compete at the same level with balanced mechanics. As technology continues to improve, cloud gaming is expected to remove hardware limitations altogether, making high-performance gaming possible on any device, anywhere in the world.

Another key development shaping the future of competitive play is the rise of AI-driven coaching and analytics. In the past, professional teams relied on human analysts and coaches to break down strategies and player performance. In 2025 and beyond, AI-powered coaching systems will provide real-time analysis, predictive decision-making models, and personalized feedback to help players optimize their performance. These tools will bridge the gap between amateur and professional players, allowing anyone with dedication and skill to refine their gameplay at an elite level.

Esports will also become more interactive for fans, transforming tournaments into fully immersive digital experiences. Virtual reality (VR) and augmented reality (AR) will allow spectators to watch matches from within the game itself, choosing different perspectives, standing next to their favorite players in virtual arenas, and even interacting with live in-game events. AI-generated real-time commentary and holographic replays will enhance the viewing experience, making esports more engaging than ever before.

Monetization and player compensation will also evolve as esports becomes more structured and financially sustainable. In the past, only the top-tier professionals earned significant incomes through tournament winnings and sponsorships. The future will see league-based salaries, revenue-sharing models, and direct fan-funded support systems, ensuring that even mid-tier players can earn a sustainable living. Blockchain technology and NFTs will further revolutionize esports monetization, allowing digital assets, exclusive skins, and tournament rewards to have real-world value.

Perhaps the most exciting change in esports is the global expansion of talent pools. With internet access improving in developing regions and mobile gaming growing in popularity, players from previously underrepresented countries will have greater opportunities to compete in international tournaments. All-Star 2025 was instrumental in breaking regional barriers, proving that talent exists everywhere, not just in traditional gaming powerhouses like North America, Europe, and South Korea.

In the coming years, esports will no longer be just a competition—it will be a full-fledged global sport, a digital-first entertainment industry, and an ever-evolving ecosystem of players, fans, and technological innovation. The future of competitive play is limitless, and we are only at the beginning of a revolution that will shape the next generation of interactive entertainment.

Chapter 10
The Future of Gaming Beyond All-Star 2025

As groundbreaking as All-Star 2025 has been, it is just one step in the ever-evolving landscape of gaming. The industry has reached an inflection point where technological advancements, player expectations, and new business models are reshaping what games can be. With innovations in AI, cloud gaming, virtual reality (VR), augmented reality (AR), blockchain, and cross-platform integration, the future of gaming is poised to be more immersive, accessible, and player-driven than ever before.

One of the most significant trends that will shape the future of gaming is AI-driven game design. While AI has already been used to enhance NPC behavior, procedural world generation, and real-time game balancing, the next wave of gaming will see AI-powered storytelling, dynamic narratives, and adaptive learning systems that personalize the gaming experience. Future titles will learn from a player's decisions, altering quests, environments, and character interactions to create completely unique gaming experiences. This means no two players will have the exact same journey, making games feel truly alive and responsive.

Cloud gaming will also play a massive role in breaking down hardware barriers. With services like NVIDIA GeForce Now, Xbox Cloud Gaming, and PlayStation Now already laying the groundwork, the future will see AAA-quality gaming available on any device, from smartphones to smart TVs, without the need for high-end consoles or gaming PCs. This shift will democratize gaming, allowing more players around the world to experience high-performance games without expensive hardware investments. As 5G and fiber-optic internet become more widespread, latency issues will decrease, making real-time multiplayer cloud gaming more viable.

VR and AR will also redefine the gaming experience by making virtual worlds more immersive than ever. While VR has been around for years, current limitations such as motion sickness, expensive headsets, and limited game libraries have prevented mass adoption. However, future VR technology will feature lighter, wireless headsets with improved field-of-view, real-time tracking, and full-body haptic feedback, making virtual worlds feel more realistic and engaging. AR, on the other hand, will integrate digital elements into real-world environments, turning everyday spaces into interactive gaming experiences. Imagine playing a game where your living room transforms into an alien battlefield, or walking through your city while seeing quests and challenges overlaid onto real landmarks.

Blockchain and decentralized gaming will also introduce new ownership models, where players truly own in-game assets. Unlike traditional games where skins, weapons, and characters are locked within a single title, blockchain-powered games will allow players to trade and transfer digital items across multiple games and platforms. This will create player-driven economies, where in-game items have real-world value, giving players more control over their gaming investments.

Beyond technology, gaming as a social and cultural force will continue to grow. The rise of metaverse-style games, player-generated content, and interactive storytelling will make gaming more than just a pastime—it will be a primary form of digital identity and social interaction. Esports will expand further, blending with traditional sports, and game-inspired experiences will become a dominant part of global entertainment.

While All-Star 2025 set new standards for competitive gaming, the next generation of games will push boundaries even further, redefining how players experience, interact, and shape the digital worlds of the future.

What Comes Next?

The future of gaming is set to undergo radical transformations, driven by cutting-edge technology, evolving player expectations, and new business models. While All-Star 2025 marked a milestone in competitive and immersive gaming, it is only the beginning of what's possible. As artificial intelligence, quantum computing, cloud gaming, and blockchain continue to evolve, the next decade will redefine gaming as an interactive, limitless, and player-driven experience.

One of the most exciting advancements shaping the future is AI-powered game design. Artificial intelligence will revolutionize gaming by creating adaptive and personalized storytelling experiences. Unlike traditional scripted narratives, future games will react dynamically to player choices, offering quests, dialogue, and world-building elements that evolve based on how each player interacts with the game. NPCs will no longer be static, robotic characters; instead, they will behave intelligently, remember past interactions, and develop unique relationships with players. This shift will make every gaming experience unique, ensuring that no two players share the exact same journey.

Another major leap forward will come with quantum computing, which promises hyper-realistic physics, infinite-world generation, and real-time AI decision-making. Today's hardware struggles with processing complex calculations for massive open-world games, but quantum computing could eliminate these limitations, making entirely destructible environments, real-time climate simulations, and planet-sized multiplayer maps possible. This would allow developers to create persistent, living game worlds that continuously evolve, driven by both player actions and AI systems that respond intelligently.

The death of hardware-based gaming is also on the horizon, thanks to cloud gaming. Traditional gaming consoles and expensive PCs may soon become obsolete, as streaming services enable players to access AAA-quality games on any device. With 5G and fiber-optic networks reducing latency, cloud gaming will allow players to enjoy high-performance gaming on smartphones, tablets, and smart TVs without the need for dedicated hardware. Subscription-based models like Xbox Game Pass and Nvidia GeForce Now are early examples of what will become the standard gaming ecosystem, where players pay a monthly fee for unlimited access to vast game libraries.

The role of blockchain and decentralized gaming will further redefine the industry by giving players true ownership of in-game assets. Currently, microtransactions lock cosmetic items and upgrades within individual games, but NFT-based economies will enable players to buy, sell, and trade their digital assets across different platforms. This will create a new, player-driven economy, where virtual items have real-world value. Blockchain technology will also introduce decentralized gaming markets, cutting out publishers and allowing players to directly exchange in-game goods, currencies, and exclusive collectibles.

Beyond technological advancements, gaming will become more integrated into everyday life, influencing social interaction, entertainment, and even professional industries. The rise of metaverse-style virtual spaces, AI-driven esports training, and VR-powered workplaces will turn gaming into a dominant form of digital existence. Ultimately, the next decade will prove that gaming isn't just an industry—it's a fundamental part of the future of entertainment, social interaction, and technology.

Emerging Technologies Shaping the Industry

The gaming industry is undergoing a technological revolution, with innovations that are set to completely transform game design, player interaction, and business models. As gaming moves beyond traditional consoles and PCs, new technologies such as artificial intelligence, quantum computing, cloud gaming, virtual reality, and blockchain are shaping the next era of immersive and accessible gaming. These advancements are not just improving graphics and gameplay mechanics; they are redefining how games are built, experienced, and monetized.

Artificial intelligence is rapidly advancing, allowing game developers to create dynamic, evolving narratives that adapt to each player's choices. Instead of static storylines, AI-driven games will be able to generate quests, dialogue, and characters on demand, making every playthrough unique. NPCs will no longer be scripted with repetitive behavior, but will instead be capable of reacting, remembering past interactions, and developing relationships with the player over time. AI will also assist in game balancing, monitoring player progress and dynamically adjusting difficulty levels to keep players engaged without frustration. This will create a more personalized and immersive gaming experience, where each player's journey feels handcrafted just for them.

Quantum computing has the potential to break the limits of what is possible in gaming, offering hyper-realistic physics, real-time environmental interactions, and unprecedented AI complexity. With quantum-level processing power, game environments will react with true-to-life precision, meaning that things like wind effects, water movement, and object destruction will be simulated in real time. Additionally, quantum computing will allow for persistent, shared game worlds where millions of players can interact simultaneously, without lag or performance drops. This technology will elevate gaming realism to new heights, making virtual worlds indistinguishable from reality in terms of physics, complexity, and interactivity.

Cloud gaming is already disrupting the industry by eliminating the need for expensive gaming hardware, making high-performance gaming available on any device with an internet connection. As 5G and high-speed fiber networks expand globally, cloud gaming will become the default method for playing games, allowing players to stream AAA titles instantly without downloading or installing them. This means that players will no longer need to upgrade their hardware every few years, as cloud servers will handle all the heavy computing power. Subscription-based gaming models will replace traditional one-time purchases, much like how Netflix and Spotify transformed the film and music industries. This shift will make gaming more affordable and widely accessible, ensuring that anyone, anywhere, can play high-end games without limitations.

Blockchain technology is also making waves in gaming, introducing true player ownership of in-game assets and decentralized gaming economies. Instead of items being locked into a single game or account, blockchain allows players to buy, sell, and trade digital assets across multiple platforms, making in-game items as valuable as physical collectibles. Players will have full control over their virtual goods, and developers will be able to create player-driven economies where digital assets hold real-world value. Blockchain technology will also introduce transparent and fraud-proof transactions, ensuring that in-game purchases are secure, traceable, and resistant to hacking or duplication.

These emerging technologies are pushing gaming into uncharted territory, creating a future where games are smarter, more immersive, and seamlessly integrated into everyday life. The industry is shifting towards limitless, player-driven experiences that will continue to evolve in ways that are almost unimaginable today.

Lessons from the Success of All-Star 2025

The success of All-Star 2025 was not just a result of innovative gameplay and cutting-edge technology; it was a masterclass in game development, player engagement, and industry evolution. The game redefined competitive gaming, esports, and digital entertainment, leaving behind valuable lessons for future developers, publishers, and the gaming community as a whole. These lessons extend beyond technical achievements, touching upon player-driven design, ethical monetization, community involvement, and sustainable game development.

One of the biggest takeaways from All-Star 2025 is the importance of listening to players and evolving based on community feedback. From the very beginning, the developers built the game with a player-first approach, integrating direct community input into balance updates, feature rollouts, and game expansions. This approach fostered trust and loyalty within the player base, proving that a game that grows alongside its community will always remain relevant. Instead of forcing unwanted mechanics or monetization strategies onto players, the development team consistently engaged with the audience through transparent communication, open beta tests, and feedback-driven patches. The result was a game that felt alive, responsive, and tailored to the evolving needs of its players.

Another major lesson from All-Star 2025 is the balance between innovation and accessibility. While the game introduced groundbreaking mechanics, AI-powered interactions, and next-level esports integration, it never lost sight of core gameplay fundamentals that made it enjoyable for both casual and competitive players. Too often, games become overly complex or intimidating for new players when they push too hard for innovation without considering usability. All-Star 2025 managed to strike a perfect balance between depth and simplicity, making it easy for beginners to jump in while offering an incredibly high skill ceiling for competitive players. The lesson here is that technological advancements should enhance, not complicate, the player experience.

The game also proved that monetization does not have to come at the expense of player trust. In an era where many live-service games have faced backlash for predatory microtransactions and pay-to-win mechanics, All-Star 2025 demonstrated that ethical monetization models lead to long-term financial success. By offering cosmetic-only purchases, fair battle pass rewards, and a transparent economy, the developers maintained player goodwill while still generating significant revenue. The lesson for future developers is clear: players will support a game financially if they feel valued and respected.

Another crucial takeaway from the game's success is the importance of cross-platform integration and cloud-based accessibility. All-Star 2025 was designed from the ground up to be playable across multiple devices, ensuring that players on PC, consoles, and mobile could compete seamlessly. This accessibility expanded its player base dramatically and set a new standard for barrier-free gaming. Future developers must recognize that gaming is no longer tied to a single platform—cross-play and cloud gaming are the future of the industry.

Ultimately, All-Star 2025 succeeded because it respected its players, embraced innovation responsibly, and built a sustainable, evolving ecosystem. It stands as a blueprint for the future of competitive gaming, proving that when developers put players first, prioritize fairness, and innovate with purpose, they create something truly legendary.

The Evolution of Interactive Entertainment

Interactive entertainment has come a long way from its humble beginnings. What started as simple pixel-based arcade games has transformed into highly immersive, AI-driven, player-centric experiences that blur the lines between reality and virtual worlds. With advancements in technology, storytelling, artificial intelligence, and real-time connectivity, gaming has evolved from a niche pastime into one of the most dominant forms of global entertainment. The journey of interactive entertainment reflects the changing relationship between technology and human creativity, shaping how we play, communicate, and even work in digital spaces.

One of the biggest drivers of this evolution has been technological advancements. The leap from 2D side-scrollers to open-world 3D environments revolutionized gaming, and today, we stand on the verge of hyper-realistic simulations powered by quantum computing, AI, and virtual reality. With the ability to render lifelike characters, dynamic worlds, and physics-based interactions, modern gaming is no longer just a form of recreation—it is a digital reality that players can actively shape. The introduction of real-time ray tracing, cloud gaming, and AI-driven storytelling has further elevated immersion, making games feel more cinematic and responsive than ever before.

Another key aspect of interactive entertainment's evolution is the rise of player-driven experiences. Unlike the early days of linear game design, where players followed a fixed storyline, today's games are built around choice, adaptability, and dynamic narratives. AI-driven game worlds now respond to player decisions in real-time, creating unique, evolving stories that are never the same twice. Procedural world generation, combined with AI-powered NPCs that learn and react, has made modern games living ecosystems where players shape their own destinies. This shift has transformed gaming from a pre-scripted experience to an interactive, ever-changing universe.

The social dimension of gaming has also undergone a significant transformation. In the past, gaming was mostly a solitary or local multiplayer experience, but today, it has become a global social network. Games like All-Star 2025 have demonstrated the power of esports, live-streaming, and in-game communities, proving that gaming is no longer just about individual achievements—it is about shared experiences and connections. Platforms like Twitch, YouTube Gaming, and virtual reality hangouts have made gaming a space for social interaction, content creation, and even professional competition. The concept of a metaverse, where players can live, work, and play in fully digital spaces, is now closer than ever to becoming a reality.

Monetization and business models have also evolved alongside interactive entertainment. Traditional one-time purchases have given way to subscription models, battle passes, and blockchain-based economies, where players own in-game assets and trade them across different platforms. The integration of NFTs, digital currencies, and decentralized marketplaces is reshaping how players interact with in-game economies, making gaming not just a hobby but a real-world economic ecosystem.

As interactive entertainment continues to evolve, it is clear that gaming is no longer just about playing—it is about living, creating, and experiencing new realities. With AI, virtual worlds, and digital social spaces advancing rapidly, the future of interactive entertainment promises to be more immersive, intelligent, and boundless than ever before.

Chapter 11
The Legacy of All-Star 2025

Few games achieve the level of influence and cultural impact that All-Star 2025 did. More than just a successful title, it became a defining moment in gaming history, setting new standards for game development, esports, player engagement, and interactive entertainment. As the gaming industry continues to evolve, All-Star 2025 remains a benchmark for innovation, community involvement, and technological excellence, leaving behind a legacy that will shape the future of gaming for years to come.

The game's impact was felt across multiple dimensions, from its revolutionary mechanics and AI-driven storytelling to its role in expanding esports and reshaping gaming culture. It wasn't just a game people played; it was a game people lived, streamed, competed in, and built careers around. By seamlessly integrating cross-platform accessibility, dynamic real-time physics, and intelligent NPC interactions, it raised the bar for what players expected from modern games.

One of the defining aspects of All-Star 2025's legacy is its influence on game development philosophy. It proved that player-driven content, evolving in-game worlds, and AI-powered experiences were not just experimental features but the future of interactive storytelling. Developers around the world took inspiration from its success, incorporating procedural storytelling, responsive AI mechanics, and immersive physics-based gameplay into their own projects. The game's open-ended narrative structure, where players shaped outcomes in a persistent universe, became a gold standard for next-generation RPGs and competitive multiplayer experiences.

Beyond gameplay, All-Star 2025 played a pivotal role in reshaping esports and competitive gaming. The game's ranked systems, AI-assisted coaching, real-time match analysis, and cross-platform tournaments revolutionized the way competitive gaming functioned. Esports organizations adopted new training methods, leveraging AI analytics to help players refine their skills. The game's franchise-based esports leagues and interactive fan participation models set a precedent for the next evolution of competitive gaming, proving that esports was not just a niche market but a mainstream global industry on par with traditional sports.

Perhaps the most remarkable part of All-Star 2025's legacy is its cultural and social impact. It wasn't just a game to be played—it became a social platform, a creative space, and a digital economy where players connected, expressed themselves, and even made a living. The game's user-generated content ecosystem, where players could design, trade, and sell in-game assets, redefined the idea of ownership in gaming. Its influence extended beyond the gaming community, shaping pop culture, fashion, music collaborations, and digital entertainment trends.

Ultimately, All-Star 2025 will be remembered not just as a technical achievement or a commercial success, but as a game that reshaped the way people experience digital worlds. Its ability to blend competitive play, immersive storytelling, and technological breakthroughs ensured that it wasn't just a product of its time, but a foundation for the future of gaming. Even as new technologies emerge and gaming continues to evolve, All-Star 2025 will remain a symbol of what happens when innovation, community, and creativity converge in perfect harmony.

How the Game Changed the Industry

The impact of All-Star 2025 on the gaming industry was nothing short of revolutionary. While many games achieve commercial success, only a handful reshape industry standards, redefine player expectations, and leave a lasting influence on game development philosophies. All-Star 2025 was one such game. It didn't just push boundaries—it shattered them, setting a new gold standard for technological innovation, competitive gaming, community-driven content, and monetization models.

One of the most significant ways All-Star 2025 changed the industry was through its integration of AI-driven mechanics and adaptive gameplay. Unlike traditional games where non-playable characters (NPCs) followed scripted behaviors, All-Star 2025 introduced AI-powered NPCs that learned from player actions and dynamically adjusted their responses. This level of intelligence made single-player and multiplayer experiences more immersive than ever before, influencing countless future game developers to integrate machine learning and behavioral AI into their own designs. It proved that games could evolve and adapt in real time, making each player's experience truly unique.

Another game-changing innovation was All-Star 2025's cross-platform accessibility and cloud gaming integration. At a time when many major titles were still locked into platform-exclusive ecosystems, this game blurred the line between console, PC, and mobile gaming, allowing players to seamlessly transition between devices without losing progress. This level of cross-play functionality became the industry standard, forcing competitors to rethink how gaming should be structured in a world where hardware limitations no longer dictate player engagement.

The game's impact on esports and competitive gaming was equally profound. All-Star 2025 didn't just introduce a new title to the competitive scene—it transformed how esports leagues were structured, managed, and monetized. With its built-in AI-driven coaching tools, automated real-time match analysis, and dynamic tournament systems, it changed how players trained, strategized, and engaged with competitive gaming. Future esports titles followed suit, integrating AI analytics and real-time feedback mechanisms to improve training and player performance. This shift led to a more data-driven approach to esports, helping professional gamers refine their skills at an unprecedented level.

The business model of gaming also underwent a transformation thanks to All-Star 2025. Unlike many live-service games that relied on aggressive microtransactions or pay-to-win mechanics, this game demonstrated that ethical monetization strategies could be both profitable and player-friendly. By focusing on cosmetic-only purchases, fair battle pass progression, and a transparent in-game economy, it proved that players were willing to spend money when they felt respected, rather than exploited. This success prompted many studios to rethink their approach to monetization, leading to a more balanced and sustainable economic model across the industry.

Perhaps the most far-reaching influence of All-Star 2025 was its community-driven content ecosystem. By allowing players to design, trade, and monetize in-game assets, it pioneered a new era of player-led content creation. This model encouraged greater player investment and creativity, fostering a thriving ecosystem of user-generated content. Many games that followed adopted similar community-driven approaches, recognizing the immense value of giving players the tools to shape their own gaming experiences.

Through its technological innovations, industry-changing esports model, ethical monetization strategies, and player-driven economy, All-Star 2025 didn't just leave its mark on gaming—it redefined what the industry could be, setting the foundation for the future of interactive entertainment.

The Impact on Future Game Development

The success of All-Star 2025 left a profound impact on how games are developed, structured, and designed, influencing future game studios, independent developers, and major publishers alike. Its technological advancements, player-centric design philosophy, and innovative business model became the blueprint for the next generation of game development, shaping everything from AI-driven storytelling to ethical monetization strategies. The game was more than just a cultural phenomenon—it was a catalyst for the evolution of interactive entertainment.

One of the most significant contributions All-Star 2025 made to future game development was the integration of artificial intelligence in game design. The game's use of adaptive AI-driven NPCs, real-time strategy adjustments, and dynamic world evolution set a new standard for game realism and interactivity. Future developers took inspiration from these innovations, pushing AI beyond basic pathfinding and scripted interactions. Games that followed adopted machine learning algorithms that allowed NPCs to react to player choices, create emergent gameplay scenarios, and evolve in complexity over time. This approach made single-player and multiplayer experiences richer, less predictable, and deeply immersive.

Another major impact was the push for cross-platform accessibility. Before All-Star 2025, many game developers struggled with segmented player bases due to hardware exclusivity, forcing users to commit to a specific platform. However, All-Star 2025 proved that seamless cross-play across consoles, PCs, and mobile devices was not only possible but highly successful in expanding player engagement and community longevity. This shift led to more studios prioritizing cloud-based gaming, universal cross-progression, and platform-agnostic multiplayer experiences, ensuring that players were no longer limited by their hardware choices.

The game's live-service model and content evolution approach also reshaped development strategies. Unlike traditional releases that required sequels or expansion packs to remain relevant, All-Star 2025 demonstrated that continuous updates, seasonal content, and player-driven events could keep a game alive for years without the need for a completely new title. This encouraged more developers to focus on long-term content plans, prioritizing sustainable, evolving experiences rather than one-time, finite narratives. The era of games as a constantly evolving platform became the new industry norm.

One of the most crucial lessons future developers learned from All-Star 2025 was the importance of ethical monetization. At a time when many studios faced backlash for predatory microtransactions and pay-to-win models, All-Star 2025 provided an example of how cosmetic monetization, fair battle pass systems, and transparent player-driven economies could be both financially successful and consumer-friendly. As a result, many studios moved away from exploitative monetization tactics, instead focusing on player trust, optional purchases, and value-driven content offerings.

Perhaps the most lasting impact of All-Star 2025 was its emphasis on community-driven content. By allowing players to create, share, and monetize their own in-game assets, it redefined the relationship between developers and their communities. Many games that followed embraced modding tools, creator marketplaces, and user-generated events, recognizing that empowering players to shape their own gaming experiences leads to longer-lasting engagement and deeper immersion.

Through AI-driven innovation, cross-platform accessibility, ethical monetization, and player-generated content, All-Star 2025 set a new foundation for game development, influencing how the industry approaches design, technology, and player interaction for years to come.

The Lasting Influence on Players and Culture

The impact of All-Star 2025 extended far beyond the gaming industry—it reshaped player experiences, influenced pop culture, and redefined the way people interact with digital entertainment. Few games manage to achieve legendary status, but All-Star 2025 did more than just entertain—it became a cultural movement, influencing not only how games are played but how they are integrated into everyday life. Its deeply immersive gameplay, community-driven content, and esports dominance left a lasting impression on millions of players, changing the way they engaged with interactive entertainment.

One of the most significant ways All-Star 2025 influenced players was through its ability to create deeply personal and dynamic experiences. Unlike traditional games with fixed narratives, All-Star 2025 allowed players to shape their own journeys, leading to unique, emergent gameplay moments that felt as if they were truly a part of the game's world. The introduction of AI-powered NPCs and dynamic storytelling gave every player a different experience, making the game feel alive and unpredictable. This fundamentally changed player expectations, making them demand more personalized, reactive, and evolving game worlds in future titles.

The game also revolutionized community engagement, making gaming more than just an individual activity—it became a shared cultural experience. Players didn't just play All-Star 2025; they streamed, created content, and built digital careers around it. Streaming platforms like Twitch and YouTube Gaming saw record-breaking viewership, with millions tuning in to watch high-level gameplay, strategy breakdowns, and creative in-game events. The rise of streamer-driven content and interactive gaming communities encouraged players to become more than just participants—they became creators, shaping how the game evolved over time. This shift in player engagement led to a broader cultural acceptance of gaming as both an entertainment medium and a legitimate career path.

Esports also saw a major transformation due to All-Star 2025. The game's high-skill ceiling, real-time analytics, and AI-assisted coaching tools set new standards for professional gaming, making competitive play more accessible and structured. Traditional sports organizations, celebrities, and global brands invested in All-Star 2025 esports, leading to massive tournament prize pools and stadium-level events. The game's popularity helped bridge the gap between traditional sports and gaming culture, further cementing esports as a mainstream competitive industry.

Beyond gaming, All-Star 2025 had a profound effect on fashion, music, and entertainment. The game's influence was seen in collaborations with global fashion brands, music artists, and

Hollywood studios, further blurring the lines between digital and physical entertainment. The in-game economy and digital fashion scene allowed players to express themselves through custom skins, exclusive items, and personalized avatars, reinforcing gaming's role as a form of self-expression and identity building.

Ultimately, All-Star 2025 left behind more than just a successful gaming legacy—it changed how people viewed and interacted with games, elevating them to an integral part of global culture. The game's influence is still felt today, shaping how players connect, compete, and create within digital worlds, proving that gaming is not just a hobby, but a cultural force that defines a generation.

Conclusion

All-Star 2025 was more than just a game—it was a cultural phenomenon, a technological milestone, and a defining moment in the evolution of interactive entertainment. It reshaped the gaming industry, pushed the boundaries of technology, and created a community-driven ecosystem that changed how players engage with digital worlds. From its groundbreaking use of artificial intelligence and dynamic storytelling to its influence on esports, monetization, and player creativity, All-Star 2025 left an enduring legacy that will continue to shape the future of gaming for years to come.

One of the most remarkable aspects of All-Star 2025 was how it blurred the lines between gaming, social interaction, and digital identity. It was no longer just about competing or progressing through levels—it became a living platform where players could express themselves, form connections, and create content that extended beyond the game itself. Whether through streaming, esports, digital fashion, or user-generated experiences, the game demonstrated that gaming was no longer just a hobby—it was an integral part of modern culture.

The game's technological innovations also set a new standard for future developers. Its AI-driven NPCs, cross-platform accessibility, and cloud gaming integration proved that gaming no longer had to be restricted by hardware limitations or pre-scripted experiences. It redefined what was possible in gaming, leading to a wave of innovation across the industry. Developers who once relied on traditional game design methodologies were inspired by All-Star 2025 to experiment with procedural storytelling, dynamic physics, and intelligent game worlds. It was a game that didn't just entertain—it challenged the industry to think bigger.

The impact of All-Star 2025 on competitive gaming and esports was equally profound. It transformed esports from a niche competitive scene into a mainstream global industry, with AI-assisted training programs, professional coaching analytics, and real-time fan engagement tools. The game's structured esports ecosystem introduced franchise-based leagues, interactive tournaments, and scalable competition formats, ensuring that competitive gaming was accessible to both amateur players and professional athletes. This evolution helped esports become a respected, financially sustainable industry, with huge sponsorships, media rights deals, and international fan engagement.

From a business perspective, All-Star 2025 proved that ethical monetization could be both profitable and player-friendly. It avoided exploitative pay-to-win mechanics and instead focused on cosmetic-based monetization, fair battle pass progression, and player-driven economies. This approach set a precedent for other game developers, proving that respecting players' financial investment leads to long-term success.

But perhaps the most enduring legacy of All-Star 2025 is its community-driven impact. It empowered players to become content creators, competitors, and storytellers, fostering a culture where gaming was about participation, collaboration, and shared experiences. It was a game built not just by developers, but by the people who played it, streamed it, and shaped its world over time.

As the gaming industry continues to evolve, All-Star 2025 will remain a symbol of what is possible when innovation, creativity, and player engagement come together. It wasn't just a game that defined a generation—it was a blueprint for the future of gaming.

www.ingramcontent.com/pod-product-compliance
Lightning Source LLC
LaVergne TN
LVHW061527070526
838199LV00009B/402